SCARLET TUNIC

On patrol with the
Royal Canadian Mounted Police
Volume 2

Robert Gordon Teather

DISCLAIMER

The events you are about to read are all true. Certain liberties have, however, been taken and events which have occurred on separate days, have been compressed into one shift.

The men and women you are about to meet are real people with whom I have worked long hard hours. I will always share with them a bond of friendship.

The victims are also real people, with whom I have shared time, space, friendship and tears. I have changed their names, however, so that they may continue to enjoy their privacy.

The names of the guilty have also been changed so that they may be protected from public scrutiny.

Sad, isn't it, that we have to protect the guilty?

PHOTO CREDITS
FRONT COVER: Kenneth K. Burton
BACK COVER: *Vancouver Province*

Copyright © 1996 Robert Gordon Teather

Canadian Cataloguing in Publication Data

Teather, Robert Gordon, 1947–
  Scarlet tunic

  ISBN 1-895811-26-0 (v.1). ISBN 1-895811-01-5 (v.2)

  1. Police patrol – British Columbia – Surrey. 2. Royal
Canadian Mounted Police. I. Title.
HV8160.S97T42 1994   363.2'32'0971133   C94-910482-5

First Edition – 1996

HERITAGE HOUSE PUBLISHING COMPANY LTD.
Unit #8, 17921 55th Ave., Surrey, B.C. V3S 6C4

Printed in Canada

2

CONTENTS

DEDICATION

To Susan, my loving wife who has always stood by my side, shared my laughter and caught my tears.

I love you, Susan.

ACKNOWLEDGMENTS

Writing these stories has been made possible by the generous support, wisdom and encouragement of many friends. To the following I will always be grateful:

Chief William J. Heckler (Retired). I thank you, Brother, for your support, your strength and your wisdom.

Leonard Krygsveld, who reached out when I was alone and gave me life's most valuable gift — friendship.

Art Downs, and his wife, Doris, who have become not just my publisher, but dear friends. Especially Art, who has always been kind and understanding. Thanks, Art, for calling me at home, late at night, just to teach me that "Grammar are important!"

Corporal Don Withers, I will not forget you, my friend.

Jack Webb, who first told the nation what it was like to be a police officer.

All members of the Royal Canadian Mounted Police, with whom I have shared long nights, tough fights, laughter and tears.

And to you, my readers. Please choose a quiet place and an open heart as you meet my family, the Modern Mounties.

4

AUTHOR'S FOREWORD

The Royal Canadian Mounted Police has a tradition that began in 1873. Since then, it has been kept alive by dedicated members who have kept their oath and pledged their lives to serve and "Maintain the Right" of Canadians. Sadly, since the birth of the RCMP, over 376 of our members have died in the line of duty. Even so, the tradition of Canada's national police force has been kept alive not only by the dedicated actions of its Police Officers, but also by television shows, movies and the postcards of today. Throughout the world, the RCMP and its colorful Scarlet Tunic have become a tradition. A trademark of Canada, if you will. A symbol of a young country, still stumbling its way into the future, but doing so with its head held high and its conscience clear.

The RCMP is, to most people, Canada's history. That is why I have written these tales. To reveal how we are still making history, how the tradition of our National Police Force lives on after nearly 125 years. To show you that we are alive and well, not just on postcards and in souvenir shops, but in police cars and in your homes when you call us. There are about 18,000 of us. We are your neighbors and we would like you to know us better.

This is a book of laughter and tears, of heroism and sadness. Such is our life and such is the secret we are told we must keep from the public. Many of us feel that the time has come to reveal the mystery behind the Scarlet Tunic and within these pages you will discover many of our secrets. Perhaps you will even discover that we are similar to you. No better, no worse. Oh, perhaps we are a bit different and I hope you will excuse this difference. It is what keeps our police family together, functioning and alive.

We are strong at times but weak at others. Often, we revel in our happiness, yet just as often we choke back tears — horribly sad tears — that we are taught never to reveal.

For this reason, when I wrote the first volume of *SCARLET TUNIC* I was concerned about the effect when the public realized that we aren't mystical beings but ordinary people no different from them. Happily, my concern was baseless. After Volume One appeared, my fears of people discovering that we had feelings like them turned to elation as the letters arrived. Oh, I was not flooded with them and the Postal Services did not have to assign a special truck just for my "fan" mail. Yet the many letters I received were very special and I have kept every one.

A lady whom I had never met wrote: "As I read each page I sobbed. When the book was finished I knew that I had looked inside a Mountie's heart — tender and compassionate. I thank God

5

for your vulnerability and transparency; for loving your wife and for keeping your sanity and sensitivity. One day I asked my son why he wanted to be a policeman. He looked at me surprised and replied 'Because I want to help people.' That is really what your book is all about."

A gentleman wrote: "I started your book 1900 hrs. Christmas Eve and concluded it at 0300 hrs. the next morning."

And the letters kept coming. From England, the United States and cities I had never heard of. I was encouraged by those I had never met.

That is why I wrote this second book. I was encouraged by countless friends, old and new, to continue telling our stories. I sat at home answering telephone calls from fellow Police Officers I had not seen in years. They were all happy with the book and, more important, they were happy that I had told the truth. Oh, I admit, my own Force had little to say about the book. I gave several copies to my supervisors and other high-ranking members of our Force. Only once did I receive an acknowledgment — a thank you. I am not sure why this lack of communication exists. Perhaps this is a hold-over of our own tradition established in 1873. The British tradition demanded a barrier be erected between Officers and enlisted men. This malice, born out of class distinction and military tradition, still continues within the RCMP. Perhaps it is indeed a sad commentary on our own Force's inability to change with the times and yet perhaps this barrier is necessary for the existence and maintenance of a paramilitary organization.

I do not know.

Yet my peers — my Brother and Sister Officers — have written and called countless times. They were all happy with the stories. You see, this is our story. It is a tale which describes what a street-cop must go through if he or she is to survive.

In this second volume I have again revealed our successes, our failures, our hearts and our souls. We are not ashamed of who we are and what we do. As you read the following chapters, I sincerely hope that you will not be ashamed of us.

I will never forget the words in one letter delivered on a cold winter day. It said: "You wrote a beautiful and powerful book."

I am thankful for such kind words. In truth, however, it is not me alone who has written these books.

The true stories you are about to read were written into history by my family — the Modern Mounties who have sworn always to "MAINTIENS LE DROIT" ("MAINTAIN THE RIGHT.")

6

CHAPTER 1

MORE MEAT FOR THE GRINDER

THE ONLY THING NECESSARY FOR
THE TRIUMPH OF EVIL IS FOR
GOOD MEN TO DO NOTHING.
EDMUND BURKE

ROYAL CANADIAN MOUNTED POLICE
DIVISION HEADQUARTERS

"You will walk through that door, stop two paces in front of the desk and stand at attention. Do you know how to stand at attention?" The speaker was Corporal Brant.

Trying my best, I straightened my spine and let both arms hang at my side.

"When I say stand at attention, I mean it!" He spoke louder this time as he explained what standing at attention meant. "You have a steel rod shoved up your arse, clear up to the top of your skull. Your knees are locked tighter than a rusty padlock on a farm gate and your arms are so straight it feels like your hands weigh a thousand pounds each. When you assume this position, you will look straight ahead and remain silent until you are spoken to! All questions put to you will be answered 'Yes, sir,' or 'No, sir!' Is that clear?"

Feeling the pain of the imaginary rod, I replied, "Yes, sir!"

"Not me you dozy little man! My name is Corporal Brant. You don't ever call me sir! You will address Inspector King as sir."

"Yes sir — Corporal."

Fifteen minutes earlier my father had dropped me off at the RCMP Headquarters in Toronto. He patiently waited outside for my return. I had wanted Dad to witness my swearing-in but he refused. "This is your first step to becoming a man," he explained. "I think you should take it without my help."

My father spoke the words quietly as he looked out the driver's side window of his 1958 red and white Dodge. Turning to me, he urged me to hurry back, he was double-parked and didn't want his son to have to give him a ticket. He briefly turned in my direc-

7

tion and said, "Good luck, son." But I was too busy opening the door and exiting the car. Had I looked into my father's eyes I would have seen tears forming. He was saying goodbye to his child.

My attention snapped back to Corporal Brant's voice as he said, "Wait here. I'll be back."

He disappeared through the office door which awaited my entrance into "manhood." A short, almost inaudible conversation took place and my name was called.

"Mister Teather. Come in here." Walking stiffly, I entered the office, stopped two paces in front of an old, worn oak desk and inserted the imaginary steel rod.

"Sir," Corporal Brant spoke to the Inspector sitting behind the desk, "may I present Mr. Robert Teather. He is here to be sworn-in this morning." Then Corporal Brant smiled ever-so-faintly and added, "More meat for the grinder, Sir."

"Do you know what it means to become a member of the Royal Canadian Mounted Police?" Inspector King asked.

"Yes, sir," I lied, then corrected myself. "No, sir."

"Well, I'll tell you. It means becoming a man. Standing up for what is right. Going to work every day with a gun on your belt and fighting with people twice as big as you. Becoming a member of the Royal Canadian Mounted Police means you are about to join a family numbered over 18,000. You will never be without a friend, without a roof over your head and never alone." I nodded. "Are you willing to pay the price?" he asked.

"Yes, sir." My answer came as a reflex action.

"Humph." He made a throaty noise. "You probably don't even know what that price is — yet you volunteer. I only hope you have it in you."

Not knowing what "it" was, I nodded and remained silent ... rigid ... at attention.

Sadly, Inspector King looked at the Corporal and acknowledged, "More meat for the grinder." Opening the top drawer of his desk, he removed a large, black leather-bound Bible. Carefully, as if it held great value to him, he held the Bible in his outstretched hand. I allowed my eyes to meet his.

"Take this Bible in your right hand," he said quietly. I held the Bible as carefully as he had. "I will ask you three questions. We call them Oaths. If you promise to keep these three Oaths, you will answer 'I do so swear.' Do you understand?"

"I swear ... I do so swear ... I...." I could feel the blood rushing to my face.

"Wait for it," he said slowly. "Look at me, son."

Our eyes met. His gaze softened and his voice became quiet,

8

as though he were sharing a great moment with me — a moment we would both remember. Our eyes remained fixed on each other's gaze. Then he spoke:

"Do you swear that you will be faithful and bear true allegiance to Her Majesty Queen Elizabeth the Second, Queen of Canada, her heirs and successors according to the law. So help you God?"

"I do so swear."

"Do you solemnly swear that you will faithfully, diligently and impartially execute and perform the duties required of you as a member of the Royal Canadian Mounted Police, and will well and truly obey and perform all lawful orders and instructions that you receive as such, without fear, favor or affection of or towards any person. So help you God?"

"I do so swear."

"Do you solemnly swear that you will keep absolutely secret all knowledge and information of which you may become possessed through your position with the Royal Canadian Mounted Police; that you will not, without due authority in that behalf, discuss with members of the Force, or any other person, either by word or letter, any matter which may come to your notice through your employment with the Royal Canadian Mounted Police. So help you God?"

"I do so swear."

"You may kiss the Bible," he concluded, still looking into my eyes.

"Huh?" I heard the words but did not understand the command.

"You may kiss the Bible," he repeated.

"Okay ... I swear ... Yes, sir!" I used all the new vocabulary I had learned as my lips pressed against the cover of the Bible.

"You're supposed to kiss it — not make love to it." Then the corners of his mouth turned up in a grin which grew to a smile and matured into a subtle laugh. Reaching out he asked, "May I have my Bible back?"

When I handed him back his Bible he paused to look at the wet lip-marks still shining on the front cover. He placed it back in his drawer and stood up. His hand reached across the desk as he said, "Welcome aboard, son. You have just joined Canada's largest and tightest-knit family. Please have a seat, I'd like to talk to you for a while."

Corporal Brant slid a chair behind me and I sat down. In the next 15 minutes the formal swearing-in ceremony changed to a friendly, informal talk. He told me I had a future with the RCMP

9

that would bring tears and laughter; that the life in this new family would be one of success and failure, pain and pleasure, happiness and sadness. I was urged to depend on other members of my new family for trust and support.

Then he added, "Oh, you will meet members of many ranks that are unjust, dishonest and downright crooked. Shun them. Avoid them, son, they are an illness that we will always try to cure. Keep your eyes and your heart open, look around for those you can trust and when you find them, rely on them. Remember the three oaths you took today — the Oath of Allegiance, the Oath of Office and the Oath of Secrecy. Here, take this." He handed me a page with the oaths neatly typed in large letters. "Keep this page and read these oaths whenever you find yourself lost, in pain or facing uncertainty." I folded the paper and placed it in my shirt pocket.

Inspector King smiled. Then after wishing me success and happiness, he pushed his chair back, stood up and walked around his desk. I stood up immediately, almost at attention. Extending his hand in friendship he said goodbye and added, "When you arrive in Regina, Saskatchewan, at our Training Academy, look up Corporal Don Withers. He's an old friend. We were troopmates. I think you will learn a great deal from him. Oh, and one thing more...." Inspector King paused briefly and gripped my hand tighter. "Ask him if he still has that Deck? Tell him an old friend misses him, would you?"

He wished me well and, as we parted, I promised to look up his troopmate, Corporal Withers.

Fifteen minutes later I sat beside my father as we started the 50-mile drive home. Very few words were spoken in that hour-long drive. Father wiped his eyes a few times but I was too young to understand. Only my father truly understood what had happened. At 20, I was too young to drink alcohol but old enough to become a police officer.

Three days later I left home. I had joined the Royal Canadian Mounted Police.

CHAPTER 2

IT SHOULD HAVE BEEN ME

EVEN A FOOL, WHEN SILENT,
APPEARS WISE

SURREY, BRITISH COLUMBIA, 15 YEARS LATER.

6:00 a.m. Twenty-seven constables sat, squint-eyed and grumpy. Pretending to be fully awake, each Police Officer held his pen in hand, poised over an open notebook.

It was dayshift briefing.

The briefing room was dimly lit and dirty. A row of steel lockers formed a barrier between our morning meeting place and the dressing room and toilets. The barrier was purely visual and the odor that crept into the room was one of dirty socks, wet leather ankle boots and urine.

To my left sat Bev, a seasoned Police Officer who held an unbeaten reputation for bravery ever since the night she had torn the ear from the head of a biker with her teeth. Although she was often referred to as our resident carnosaur, she usually tried to downplay the incident, stating she was just out for a snack that night.

Rod, the senior Police Officer in our zone, sat to my right. He rubbed his eyes sleepily, first with his knuckles then the heels of his hands. He was trying to wake up. The door to the briefing room swung open and we all looked up.

"Good morning, gentlemen and ladies!" Our Watch Commander, Sergeant Denis, walked into the room and took his place at the head table. Opening a folder, he began the briefing.

"First order of business, for those of you who are interested, Constable Higgins is still in the hospital, Intensive Care Unit. He has not regained consciousness since being admitted and the Doctors aren't too happy."

"Higgy?" I leaned sideways and spoke to Bev. "What the hell happened?"

"Shut up, Teather." Denis interrupted my private conversation. "You got something to say, say it later. You should try keeping your

11

mouth shut for a change. It's always safer to keep your mouth shut and let everyone wonder about your intelligence, than open it and remove all doubt." Our Watch Commander took great delight in embarrassing his men in public. I fought back once after his tongue had cut me to ribbons, in front of the Watch, but I succeeded only in making a permanent enemy. I bowed my head in submission and stopped talking.

"Like I was saying, Higgins is still in a coma after the beating he received yesterday. Brain-swelling they call it. Those of you who think you're tough enough to take on a 240-pound mental patient alone can share a hospital bed with him. Maybe I'm stupid or something, but you have portable radios. Use them!"

"Ya, he's stupid," Bev whispered. "Been so long since he's been on the road he's forgotten how shitty our portables are." I nodded. "Transmission is so bad we can't even talk to ourselves," she added.

Sergeant Denis pierced Bev's ears to the wall with one glance, then continued with the briefing.

"ITEM #1 on today's briefing: The Miami Bureau of Fire and Arson Investigations has issued a bulletin and I'll read it." He paused to adjust his glasses. 'Pluorolastomec, a material used to make brake seals and fuel pipes in motor vehicles, may become dangerous after it has been burned. After a vehicle fire, this material melts into a highly corrosive acid which, if it gets onto the skin, cannot be removed. The only treatment is amputation.' Maybe we should put some of that in your mouth, Teather." He finalized his insult. "In addition to this nice polymer, we are also advised that electronic ignition modules have been found to contain a chemical which can, if allowed to contact the skin, cause cancer."

Rod butted his cigarette, shook his head and quietly added, "Ain't nothing safe these days?"

"ITEM #2: Bill C-17, the Budget Implementation Act received Royal Assent and became law on June 15th. All salaries of all members up to the rank of and including Superintendent will remain frozen within the RCMP for the next four years." He looked up from his paper and added, "This, however, does not affect pay negotiations for Provincial or Municipal Police Departments."

"ITEM #3," he continued in a voice as ineffective as our pay negotiations. "You will all find, in front of you, a list of eight vehicles which have been stolen overnight. B.O.L.F. all of them." Rod flicked his briefing paper over and said in a barely audible voice, "He means Be On the Lookout For. Gimme a break!"

Sergeant Denis continued, "Gentlemen, let's try not to be dis-

12

couraged about our wage freeze. We're making pretty good money and we all have a steady job."

"Excuse me, Sarge," Rod spoke out loud for all to hear. "You make pretty good money — not us. And as far as a steady job...." His face became sad as he looked at Sergeant Denis, "Tell that to Higgy. If he ever wakes up."

The members of "C" Watch cleared their throats, providing an audible and collective support for Rod. The room held 27 Constables ranging in service from 22 years to two new recruits from our Training Academy. We were Brothers and Sisters who shared long nights, hard fights, laughter and death. Wage freezes could not tear apart our family, although from time to time displays of solidarity such as "throat clearing" reminded both supervisors and management that they had left the family when they traded in their police cars for desks. Only a few senior Police Officers remained as family members.

"ITEM #4:" Sergeant Denis continued as the sound abated. He spoke louder and the room became quiet. "There will be a retirement party for Sergeant Schlitz, your former Watch Commander. It will be held this Friday night starting at 1800 hours in the White House. Sorry, but I'm not sure if I'll be able to attend."

"We'll really miss you." A sarcastic, anonymous voice drifted towards the head table. "As if you were invited," another voice said softly.

"And one small additional item." Sergeant Denis looked out over the room as he read from the clipboard. "Rank and file members of this detachment will, heretofore, consider the executive washroom on the second floor as OFF LIMITS!" He emphasized the last two words and the room broke into laughter. "I don't suppose anyone here knows why?" The laughter subsided and the room regained its formal poise. No answer, however, was given.

"That's it, gentlemen. Collect your things and hit the road."

In a flurry, our BOLF notices were scooped up and 27 men and women tried to fit through the door at once. We were all eager to leave the office and "hit the road." We were street cops and felt insecure and unwanted around the office.

I met Bev at the Duty Constable's window. She had signed out her shotgun and was arguing ownership of a pen with the Police Officer on the other side of the counter. "Give me that pen or I'll leave this office with four shells instead of five." She kissed the barrel of her gun. Placing her pen back into her shirt pocket she turned to leave.

"Bev!" I called. "Wait up!" Quickly, I signed out my shotgun and portable radio and ran after her.

13

"What happened to Higgy?" I felt sick. Constable Higgins had offered to exchange shifts for me the day prior and had worked my shift so that I could keep a date with an old friend.

I had gone fishing.

"Bruce got tangled up with an M.H.A." She used the letters we knew stood for Mental Health Act. "It was Crazy Fred Zurley. They just let him out last week and nobody has been supervising his medication. Well," Bev continued, "Higgy's portable wouldn't reach out when he called for help. Sharon recalled him calling in his 10-7 when he arrived at the Zurley residence but she heard nothing from Higgy after he turned off his car and went inside. After he had been 10-7 on the call for about 20 minutes, Rod and I went to see what the problem was."

"And....?"

"When we arrived at the house we found Higgy lying on the floor, bleeding from his ears. He was still semi-conscious, calling for back-up. He still had his portable radio case in his hand, but it was empty. Crazy Fred's wife was cowering in the corner and Fred was trying to call God on Higgy's portable radio."

Bev's eyes teared as she continued. "The bastard beat him, Bob. Beat him with his own goddamned portable. Higgy had unloaded his gun, knowing he was going to Crazy Fred's house, but he got beaten with his own friggin' portable." Bev sniffed, "Now he's...." She shrugged her shoulders, bowed her head, turned and walked away.

"Damn. Should have been me," I said as I picked up my duty bag, cradled the shotgun between its two handles and walked down the corridor.

"You're right!" Sergeant Denis said. He had been listening to our conversation.

I paused, turned to him and said, "Sarge, the way I see it, the only problem here is the spelling of your name."

"Excuse me?"

"Ya. The spelling of your name. The first letter is all-wrong."

I turned and walked to the parking lot. My police car, 5 Bravo 23, sat quietly waiting to take me on another tour of duty. I hated day shift — and this one was turning out to be the worst of all.

Silently, I walked across the parking lot, promising myself to visit Higgy.

It should have been me.

14

CHAPTER 3

START OF SHIFT

THE SADDEST WORDS OF GODS AND MEN
ARE IN THE PHRASE,
"IT MIGHT HAVE BEEN."

I stood at the back of the blue and white marked police car and shook my head. Day shift.

I hated working days. Nothing ever happened, nothing was ever learned and the only work for street cops was usually found in attending residential and business break-ins that had occurred through the night. Yesterday was an exception, however, and as much as I wanted to take the day back, to take the call that had put Higgy in the hospital, I couldn't.

I fished the car keys from my gunbelt, and opened the trunk lid for a routine visual inspection. Road flares, first-aid kit, spare tire and today's newspaper purchased by my night-shift friend and left in the trunk as a gift. I flung my duty bag into the trunk and slammed the lid.

Walking around the car, I inspected it and tried to look through the dirt for new scratches or dents to report. There were none and I entered in my notebook "5 Bravo 23 checked, okay." The dirt which had become stuck to the side panels, fenders and roof of the vehicle was another matter, however. It reminded me of how I felt.

I could not shake Higgy from my mind. I felt dirty — like the police car.

Guilt is a great punisher.

Opening the driver's door I flung my tired, worn leather briefcase onto the passenger's seat and winced as it almost bounced onto the floor. Reaching into my patrol jacket pocket, I retrieved a handful of shotgun shells and loaded Big Bertha. Loaded shotguns were not allowed inside the police station since the day Constable Randal had blown a hole in the Watch Commander's office. "Hey, I'm the Duty Constable," he said in defense. "It's my duty to ensure all firearms signed in are unloaded."

As a reward for his ingenious "Inspection Technique" he was

15

issued a written reprimand and reminded that "Pulling the trigger of a loaded firearm is an unsafe manner in which to ensure it will be safely stored." Carl Randal accepted the reprimand without comment.

I could feel the coldness of the shotgun in my hand. I gripped it tighter as I cursed the system that gave Crazy Fred his freedom and took away Higgy's. The pain and the guilt that I felt because of Bruce Higgin's injury weighed heavy on my conscience. The emotion was a combination of the hatred I had for Fred Zurley and the sadness I held for my fallen friend. I felt sick and confused.

I got into my car, reached under the dash and pulled on a hidden toggle switch. SNAK. The metal gate of the shotgun rack released and I placed the long gun in its nest, silently praying it would remain there for the next 12 hours.

The silver key slid into the ignition lock and 5 Bravo 23 came alive. "Let's see now," I thought out loud. "Fuel tank's full, battery's charging, and all the signal lights are working." Looking down, I could see my police radio light up, briefly flashing the message "Self-Test," then displaying "Channel-1," our dispatch channel. It was a new radio system. Computer Aided Dispatch (CAD) meant that even if I keyed my microphone and said nothing, Sharon, our radio operator, would see my car number "5 Bravo 23" displayed on her computer screen.

None of us liked this feature that announced our car number before we called it in. It had stifled the "Midnight Poet," a member of our watch who, when appropriate, graced our airwaves with a short limerick describing police work as he saw it. We all recognized his voice but in keeping with our own Code of Silence, never revealed it to our superiors. Since the introduction of CAD, he had to resort to using his portable. Portables bypassed the computer-integrated system but due to their unreliable range, did not give our resident poet the exposure or notoriety he sought. This defect was corrected, however, the night we heard:

> *"I'm sure you all can hear me*
> *I'm sitting in a place,*
> *Where my radio-waves*
> *And funny words*
> *Will smack you in the face!*
>
> *"You see, the CAD can't stop me*
> *My words please never doubt,*
> *So tell ol' Sergeant Denis,*
> *I think his luck's run out!"*

16

"Ksshhht!" My radio announced an incoming message as its red light flashed. "Ksshhht! Surrey, all cars, radio test Sierra Delta." Sharon was warning us that Sierra Delta was in the radio room and it would be wise to keep our transmissions to a formal level. Sierra Delta was Sergeant Denis. The phonetic equivalent of the first letters was always used to flag his name.

"5 Bravo 23 is 10-8." I signalled our dispatch that I was on shift and clear to take calls.

"10-4 Bravo 23." Sharon answered with all the formality that Sergeant Denis expected.

"I'll be in Zone 2 today, Sharon. Just finishing off my vehicle check and I'll be clear in one minute."

"10-4, Bobo." She used the nickname that had been officially assigned to me after a public reaming-out from our former Watch Commander, Sergeant Schlitz. He had accused me of assuming the role of "Watch Clown" after I had hung a sign on the rear bumper of his police car. It read "Student Cop." From that day on, I would be called Bobo by those whom I was close enough to share friendship. Sharon's familiarity told us that Denis had left the radio room. Denis behaved like a robot. Each morning he followed a fixed schedule that was more habitual than intellectual. He never deviated from it. Each morning he would walk through the radio room, glance at the dispatch screens, pretending he understood what they meant, then walk through the door into his office where he would sit and read policy and drink coffee. Policy was very important to a Non-Commissioned Officer, more commonly referred to as an NCO. Denis was no longer a street cop. Written policy was his only reference — his only measure to ensure all was well.

Slowly allowing Bravo 23 to creep ahead, I pulled up tight under his window and hit the small red button which controlled the car's siren.

"Woop Wee Yooo." It was an unkind game we played on our new Watch Commander. A cop should never forget the sound of a siren and daily we reminded Sergeant Denis of its sound. Besides, there was a free breakfast awaiting the first member of our watch who could make Denis spill his coffee.

Raising the microphone to my lips I called, "5 Bravo 23's clear for calls. Sorry 'bout the siren, I thought the Federal System was turned off." I pretended to apologize to Sharon, knowing that Sergeant Denis was listening to the conversation. A monitor had been installed on his desk and he would hear an apology for this horrible mistake.

"Bravo 23 copy," Sharon responded, then added, "Message received."

17

Message received was the code response I had been waiting for. It worked! I was the first on the watch to succeed. I would later learn that Denis had spilled coffee on his shirt, pants and his newspaper.

"Bravo 11, Bravo 23," Bev's voice called. "I'm buyin' breakfast. Name the location."

"Brave 23 and Bravo 11 stand-by, I have a priority...." Bev's voice was cut short by Sharon. Her voice tone and words had the effect of fingernails on a chalk board. She had interrupted our private conversation with an abrupt message. Bev and I could sense the urgency as we waited for our first call of the day. Briefly, I wondered what could be so important she would send us both?

"Bravo 23 and Bravo 11, ready to copy?" I pulled my notebook from my shirt pocket and pushed the yellow detail button on my radio, signalling my readiness to accept the first call of the day. Sharon sounded serious. A faint "Ksshhht" told me that Bev had also pushed her detail button.

"Bravo 23 and 11, we have just had a call from Dr. Harrington at Surrey Memorial Hospital. He reports a young girl has just been brought into Emergency by her mother. The complaint is sexual assault. Your E.T.A.?"

"Five minutes," Bev announced.

"I'll be there in 10," I replied.

"10-4," Sharon responded. "Time out is zero-six-fifteen hours." I jotted the time in my notebook and returned it to my shirt pocket.

I knew that we wouldn't be able to interview the victim until the emergency room doctor had spoken to her. In addition, she would need an extra few minutes to allow her nerves to settle. The extra time would allow me to do something first.

Pulling out of the police parking lot, I drove across the street to the White House, an old abandoned house which the Municipality had donated to our detachment. One year's work, and a few gallons of paint had the old house restored. Although the building was officially referred to as the Surrey RCMP Recreation Club, it was known to everyone simply as the White House. It was our after-hours, home-away-from-home where we often met to review our day's activities, tell stories and, sometimes, shed a tear or two.

Throwing the gear selection lever into park, I reached into my briefcase and retrieved an old cotton handkerchief. Wrapped within the folds of this cocoon was a deck of 52 home-made, handwritten cards. I looked at the initials "D.W." stitched on the corner of the handkerchief and solemnly unwrapped the contents.

As I held the 52 cards in my hand, the present blurred. My

18

mind drifted back to my days at the RCMP training academy ... to memories of an old friend ... and to a last good-bye:

It was mid-December in Regina, Saskatchewan. The sky was blacker than the inside of a bat's armpit, save for the stars that pierced the darkness. As I looked up I realized that the stars were shining with light that had left them thousands of years ago. Training was tough and the stars seemed as far away as my graduation. I had just finished gym and completed the final requirements needed in order to graduate from the Police Academy. Corporal Don Withers, our academic instructor, had summoned me to the parade square, to a meeting in the frigid, prairie air.

It was a meeting that would live with me for the rest of my life.

Standing in the cold, I could feel the hairs inside my nose freeze with every inhalation and thaw with each warm breath. Looking up at the night sky, Corporal Withers reminded me that the stars which God had hung in the sky that night were the same stars which guided the Roman Centurions on their campaigns some 2,000 years ago. He explained how the ancient Romans had come upon the magic ratio of one Centurion for ever 500 citizens; that discipline and camaraderie were necessary for a legion to survive far from home; that thousands had died fighting for what they believed was right.

At the side of the parade square, a cairn had been erected in memory of our fellow Police Officers who had fallen in the line of duty. Silently we stood there, each of us paying our respects and wondering if the price our Force asked of us was too high.

Corporal Withers, in the space of a mere half hour, had told me everything I needed to know about becoming a Police Officer. He warned me never to sell my soul in exchange for a uniform, always to stand above the corruption and dishonesty I would encounter and to respect my own gun.

"I have seen statistics," he said bluntly, "that reveal a very disturbing fact."

"Like?"

"We have more members of the Royal Canadian Mounted Police die by their own hand than are murdered on duty." He leaned forward and wiped the snow from one of the plaques. "Your gun is more dangerous to you than a half-crazed, drug-withdrawn maniac."

He paused for a moment, then added, "I'd like to show you those statistics but they're held secret. Our Force does not want its members to understand that suicide is our greatest enemy. They do not want to tell you that simple fact because it would reveal a grave fault at the highest of offices."

19

"What kind of fault?" I asked.

"Our Force asks more of its members than any other Police Force in Canada. We operate under the lowest of Police Officer-to-Civilians ratio, have the worst pay bargaining and benefits committee, and are the only Police Force in Canada which is restricted by policy to one-man cars." Corporal Withers walked around the cairn and carefully wiped the snow from each plaque. "And sometimes we pay the price."

"Doesn't sound like I've made a very wise choice in careers," I said, trying to smile.

"Oh, you have!" He turned sharply and looked directly at me. His voice became positive — enthusiastic. "In the future...." He looked skyward and greeted the stars with open arms. "...in your future, you will experience the happiest of times and the most rewarding life possible." Then he looked at the snow that he had just brushed onto the ground. "And you will endure the saddest of times."

His eyes teared but my young, eager, brain-washed mind attributed it to the cold wind.

"Here, take these." He reached into his pea-jacket pocket and produced a deck of white cards. "These will see you through as they have me."

Corporal Withers explained that late one night, in the barracks just before graduation, he and a troopmate had each made a deck of cards. On each card they had written a truism, a saying that would guide them through the long nights and lonely calls. The day before graduation they had exchanged decks and promised to read a card at the beginning of each tour of duty. The truth contained on each card would then be applied to the problems they would encounter on that specific shift.

"Take these, please." He gave me his deck. "And remember what I have taught you. It is the teaching that should live on, not the teacher."

I will always remember that cold, frozen winter night. I will always remember Corporal Don Withers' words. I will always remember the day I learned that six months after he had left the Academy, a bullet tore into his chest and ended his life.

Adios, Don. Adios, my friend.

The feel of the cotton handkerchief and the Deck of cards brought me back to the present as I unwrapped the memory of Corporal Withers. I had kept a promise. At the beginning of each tour of duty the cards spoke to me with a message that would guide me through the next 12 hours.

20

The messages were both serious and humorous and each card, each saying, held an infinite number of meanings. The Deck I held in my hand was not the one Don Withers had given me that cold winter night. I had since returned that Deck to his troopmate, my former NCO, Sergeant Schlitz. In return, he had given me Withers' Deck, the one that he had held in his briefcase for many years.

The Deck had magical properties. It could soothe jangled nerves, cheer a hurting soul and foretell the future. Such was the magic that my academic instructor had left me. He lived within this Deck of hand-written cards and would speak to me whenever I asked a question:

As directed, one cold Regina night I shuffled the Deck, cut it once and, before turning over the top card, asked it a question.

"What can you teach me today, Don?"

Turning over the top card, I read:

"Born out of sharing, miracles are natural.
When miracles stop occurring —
something has gone wrong."

As I wrapped and placed the Deck in my patrol jacket pocket, I wished I could share my injured friend's hospital bed. Bruce Higgins was injured and I felt guilty. I should have been the Police Officer dispatched to Crazy Fred's house yesterday. Sucking in the cool morning air I prayed for a miracle, then drove off into a sunrise that I hoped promised a routine day.

It was to be far from routine.

CHAPTER 4

RAPE

*COURAGE IS THE FIRST OF HUMAN
QUALITIES BECAUSE IT IS THE QUALITY
WHICH GUARANTEES ALL OTHERS.*
Winston Churchill

Leaving behind the memories of Don Withers, I watched the White House disappear in my rear view mirror as I drove to my first call of the day.

Sexual Assault! It was today's polite way of saying rape.

"Bravo 23's 10-6, last call." I acknowledged that I was now 10-6, busy on my last call. Sharon would enter the message onto her status screen and avoid assigning any further calls to Bravo 23 until I had cleared from the hospital.

"What's your 10-20, Bob?" Bev called, asking my location. She did not want to walk into the emergency room alone. Standard procedure dictated that, if possible, we walk in together. A show of strength meant a promise of safety to the victim. In truth, however, Bev and I needed each other as much as the rape victim needed us. Odds were, she would never have to be exposed to another rape in her entire life. Bev and I, on the other hand, would see dozens and whether we wanted to or not, would store each one inside us until the day we had no more room.

"I'm just coming up Stinky Barn Hill. Should be at Surrey Memorial Hospital in five minutes. Meet you in the West parking lot?"

"I'll wait for you," Bev promised.

As I crested Stinky Barn Hill, named after the two pig farms which were located on either side of the road near its crest, I watched the pigs roll in the mud and straw as I drove by. Sadly, I wondered if they knew what fate held in store for them. They looked happy. Briefly, I remembered the advice printed on one of the cards I carried with me:

*"There is nothing between birth and death,
except to enjoy the interval."*

22

"Smart pigs," I thought as I crested the hill and turned down a street that would take me to a room filled with doctors, nurses, and tears.

"I'm 30 seconds away, Bev. What's your 10-20."

"Southwest corner," she replied. "Have you forgotten we have our own parking here?"

In my own self-pity I had forgotten the freshly painted yellow lines that announced "POLICE PARKING ONLY."

As I pulled into the parking lot, I reached forward to my car's radio and pushed the yellow button labelled "RTT." (Request To Talk.)

"Bravo 23, go ahead." Sharon acknowledged the request.

"23 and 11, 10-7 S.M.H." I called in stating that Bev and I would be out of our vehicles at Surrey Memorial Hospital.

"Great way to start the day," Bev announced as she approached my police car. "What do we know about this? Is it a family affair, a hooker with a no-pay customer dispute or should we be concerned?"

Bev echoed the callousness that grew within. It was not a nice comment but it was necessary for survival. Most complaints of sexual assault fell into one of two categories. The first occurred during a divorce or separation when women often discovered that an accusation of sexual abuse against their estranged husband was an effective tool to guarantee custody of their children. Through careful interrogation, very young children could be seeded with vague, dream-like memories involving them and their father in a sexual tryst. Whether the memory was real or fabricated did not usually matter.

The father, no matter how noble, would be destroyed physically, emotionally and spiritually by the accusation. Suicide was not uncommon in this type of occurrence. Police Officers hated being used in cases where it could never be ascertained if the sexual encounter happened or was just a memory implant. There were never winners in such cases. The father would be blamed for the crime and society would instantly find him guilty. The mother would be blamed initially for allowing it to happen, but forgiven because "it was not her fault." The child would live with horrible, life-scarring memories of something that may not even have happened.

The second classification of sexual assault that caused the anger of most members was the complaint made by prostitutes. Often a prostitute, after a price quarrel with a client, attempted to use the police as her own personal collection agency. It was not uncommon for a client, or "John" as they were called, to claim he'd received "damaged goods" or "insufficient packaging" and refuse

23

to pay after delivery of her sexual favors. When this situation occurred, we felt dirty. We were Police Officers, not collection agencies for women offering their bodies for hire.

On occasion, a prostitute would rent herself out to a John who became violent, injuring or even murdering her. The days had long since passed when this violence was considered a "hazard of the trade." Even though the "victim" was one of questionable moral values, any indication of violence commanded our full attention, as well as our sympathy. A prostitute was, by definition, a criminal not unlike a shoplifter or peeping-Tom. Their crime may exact punishment by the courts, but physical violence was not part of the program.

Still, there were mixed emotions amongst the law enforcement profession. Prostitutes knowingly break the law, yet run to the police when their illegal activities cause them pain. It was a dirty situation for all. Society had rewritten the laws, introduced new cultural values and, somewhere in the shuffle, the real victims were lost.

"Let's go see," I suggested as we walked toward the Emergency entrance. "The way Sharon gave this one to us, I think we might have a genuine case here."

"In other words, you mean a bad one?"

"Ya. A bad one. Sharon sounded concerned and it was reported by Dr. Harrington. He's the best there is. I still remember the time he gave 'Samantha Two Cups' a valium and told her she should either lower her skirt or her prices."

"Samantha still working?" Bev asked.

"Yup. She's offering the Full Meal Deal for $25."

"Wow," Bev smiled. "Imagine that! A Big Mac and a side of thighs for only $25!" We laughed briefly then walked through the glass doors into the hospital.

A large sign posted inside the door read:

"Emergency - Red Line
Cafeteria - Green Line
Radiology - Blue Line
Information - Black Line"

We followed the red line until Dr. Harrington waved and motioned us to follow him. We walked behind the Nurses' station and into a small room which held three chairs, a puny desk and a telephone. Dr. Harrington took his seat behind the desk while Bev and I sat down in silence and waited for him to speak.

"What do we have, Bill?" I asked. I had known him for many years and in private I never called him Doctor and he never called me Constable. We were friends.

24

Removing his glasses, he rubbed his eyes until we could hear them squish. Then, red-eyed, he told us what we did not want to hear.

"Goddamned brutal." He looked at his notes then made eye contact with us. "Goddamned horrible." He rephrased his assessment. A pause followed. Somewhere between 30 seconds and an eternity, he wiped his eyes, swallowed and tried to regain control.

Doctor Harrington looked at his notes and read: "I have been presented with a young girl of 13 years who has claimed she was picked up on her way to school this morning by an unknown male driving a large black vehicle." He paused but did not look up. "This young girl states the man jumped from his vehicle, forced her into his car and threatened to kill her if she moved or screamed. She then advises that he drove her to somewhere that smelled very bad and was near a large bridge ... where ... where he...."

Doctor Harrington weakened and allowed the pain to show. "Where he ... he removed her clothes and beat her. He beat her and he raped her." He looked at us over his desk. "The son-of-a-bitch beat her, raped her, beat her and raped her. She's taken six stitches in her face, four on the top of her head and I think her arm's broken." He partially regained his composure. "I'll have the film back from Radiology in a few minutes."

"Broke her arm?" Bev asked.

"Want to see the tire marks where he drove over her after throwing her out of the car?" Bill asked quietly. He knew we would have to witness the injuries and have photographs taken.

"In a minute," Bev said as she made an entry into her notebook. "Where was she found?"

"That's the kicker." He shook his head. "After the bastard ran over her, he picked her up again and had a second go at her. Then he makes her put her clothes back on and drove her to school. Dropped her off about a block away."

"Damn," I swore. "We got no crime scene."

"Except for her." Bill reminded me that he had yet to complete his Rape Protocol. "Maybe I'll obtain some evidence from her." He closed his file folder, drew in a deep breath and added "Sorry — I know you hate these as much as I do."

"Excuse me, Doctor." A young woman's face peered into the room. "Radiology results are back from the lab."

"Thanks. I'll be right out." He stood up. "Time for me to be a doctor again. Healing wounds is easy. I just wish I could heal the scars that followed."

Bev and I followed Dr. Harrington down the hall to where a large lit panel held the X-rays. Gazing at the black and white negatives, I confessed to not being able to see a break.

"See this dark line?" With his pen, Dr. Harrington traced a short dark hairline near the center of the single upper-arm bone. "A hairline fracture of the humerus. I'll have to set it."

"Looks painful," Bev commented.

"Not really. The soft tissue damage and swelling will keep her awake for a few nights though. There's a lot of bruising and some bleeding."

"You can tell all that from the X-ray?" Bev asked.

"No, experience," he answered. "You want to question her before or after the examination?"

"After." I looked at Bev. "Let's let the doctor do what he has to do. We'll give the victim time to settle down before questioning her."

"The victim has a name, Bob," Bill said in a soft voice. "It's Penny, but they call her Scooter."

"Scooter?"

"Scooter," the doctor said. "She's young, blond and has the face of an angel. Scooter." He swallowed and took a deep breath. "Scooter came in first this year in her Summer School track competition trials. If only she had enough warning — she could've out-run the dirt-bag that did this to her."

"Scooter." Bev spoke out loud as she entered the name into her notebook. Bev was meticulous with her notebook. Times, dates, names, descriptions — everything she did, saw or heard was recorded. We often made fun of her and accused her of buying shares in the company that printed our notebooks.

But as I watched her and her notebook, I knew that if we were to solve this crime Bev's notes would be critical.

"Scooter. Her real name is Penny. Her file is at the Nurses' station. Why don't you two go for coffee. Give me a half hour to finish the examination, then c'mon back. I'll keep her and her Mom in the Quiet Room until you return." I nodded in agreement. "Oh, sorry to hear about Higgy. I dropped in on him this morning. He's scheduled for an MRI scan this morning. You know, Magnetic Resonance Imaging, that new machine we have. It sort of takes a picture of the brain, then slices it up so you can see any internal bleeding or injury."

"Yes, I've heard of it," I said. I was not feeling like a technical lesson on the newest scientific medical tool. I wanted to know how my friend was doing. "Any idea how he's doing? Any idea at all?" I asked.

"Bob, I threw away my crystal ball years ago. Seen minor ailments kill people and terminal cancer go into spontaneous remission. Bruce is ... well ... he's got the best doctors in the hospital car-

26

ing for him. I can't say anymore 'cause I don't know. I'm sorry. I'll check in on him later. He's in Four-West. I better go. Scooter's waiting."

"Wanna see Bruce?" Bev asked.

"Yes. Alone if you don't mind."

"I understand. Look, Bob, please don't eat yourself up over this...."

"Leave it alone!" I interrupted her compassion. "Just leave it alone."

"I'll be in the cafeteria." Bev said as she turned to walk away. "Say hi to Higgy for me."

"Okay." I turned and walked to the elevator.

Entering the elevator alone, I pushed a black button and waited until the door opened to a sign which read "Four-West. I.C.U." You did not have to be a genius to know "I.C.U." meant Intensive Care Unit. As a Police Officer I had walked these halls many times and visited many people — victims of serious motor vehicle accidents, beatings, shootings and attempted suicides.

But never to visit a friend.

"The last door on the left," a voice spoke. I had never met the nurse before but she knew why I had arrived. "He's not supposed to have any visitors. I'll warn you when the doctor comes."

"Thanks, Jane." I read her name on the small gold nameplate she wore on her breast.

It was a small room. Quiet and dim. The venetian blinds were drawn and except for the faint padding of nurses' feet on the tile hallway outside the door, the air was still.

Bruce lay near motionless. His chest rose and fell, his breath slow and shallow. A nasal cannula snaked its way from behind his head and its two clear, plastic prongs made a slight hissing noise as they vented oxygen into his nose. An I.V. stand stood sentry over the bed and electrodes from a heart monitor decorated his bare chest.

I pulled up a chair and sat by my friend, not knowing what to say. After a few minutes, I found myself talking, hoping beyond hope that he might hear me and open his eyes. Reaching out, I took his hand and held it in mine.

"Hey, Higgy, it's me. Bob. Drew a rough shift for me didn't ya, buddy." My throat tightened. "Higgy, you can't do this. You gotta open your eyes. You gotta." I gripped his hand tighter. "I'm sorry, buddy. I'm sorry. You got no family 'cept us. No one to visit you. Heck, I'll go rent Samantha Two-Cups if that'll wake you up?"

I rambled on. Then I ran out of words. Bruce had worked a shift for me and was rewarded with an injury he might never recov-

27

er from. There was nothing I could do to change what had happened or the loss of control I felt, mixed with sorrow.

"Higgy. Just wake up for me will ya'? You open those peepers and I'll buy you coffee for the rest of your life. Got that, Higgy? Coffee! For the rest of your life! Hell, I'll even deliver it to you no matter where you are." Then I rested my forehead against the chrome railing and added, "Please, Bruce. Please wake up." Closing my eyes, I prayed for a miracle.

Higgy's hand remained motionless.

"Doctor's, coming," Jane's voice echoed softly.

Carefully I laid Bruce's arm by his side, exited the room and turned sharply through another door into the stairwell.

I walked down the stairs slowly, drying my eyes and mentally promising Bruce I would be back later. As I returned to the cafeteria my mind wandered from Higgy's room to the one where Scooter and her mother waited for Bev and me. It was a strange journey back to the hospital cafeteria. A journey full of regret, sadness and fear. I regretted having allowed Bruce to work a day shift for me while I went fishing — and I feared the future I saw waiting for him.

It was a long walk to the cafeteria. Long and lonely.

"How's Bruce?" Bev asked as I sat across the table from her.

"No change."

"Sorry. Any word from the doctors?"

"No."

"Still eating you up, isn't it?" Bev knew how I felt.

"Yes."

"Well, shake yourself. We've got a job to do and I need help. Scooter needs our help and as long as you slop around in that self-pity you're oozing, we'll never catch the bastard that brutalized her. Shake yourself, Bob. Higgy will be okay for now."

I nodded and drank the remainder of her coffee.

"Help yourself," she said, smiling sarcastically as I returned her empty cup to the table.

"Thanks."

Opening her notebook, Bev filled me in on Scooter's abduction and rape. She had read Scooter's medical file and recorded much of the information for our review: "Penny Allison Fairchild. Age 13. Attending Gold Creek summer school on a special athletic program. She is enrolled in an art class from 7:00 am until 10:00 then she joins the track team. She has set three Provincial track records for her age group so far this year."

Bev turned the page in her notebook. "Mother's name is Michelle, age 32 — father's name is Pierre. They're separated.

28

Scooter is an only child. Father lives up-country and hasn't been notified yet."

I copied the details into my notebook.

"Bob?" Bev looked across the table.

"Yes?"

"What would that Deck of yours say about this situation?"

"Funny you should ask." I reached into the breast pocket of my patrol jacket. Removing the handkerchief, I shuffled then cut the Deck. Turning over the top card, we read:

It takes both rain and sunshine
to make a rainbow.

"I'd say we got some work to do," Bev announced. "Ready?"

"Let's go." We pushed our chairs back and left the cafeteria.

Two minutes later we entered the Emergency Ward and were summoned with a wave to Dr. Harrington's tiny office.

"Here's the rape kit." He shoved a white styrofoam container across his desk. "I've sealed, initialed and dated it. All ready for the Forensic Crime Detection Laboratories." Bev took possession of the box and entered into her notebook the date, time and names of all present when the transfer of evidence took place.

"God, I hate these examinations," Bill said. "It's bad enough she was raped three times, beaten and run over by a car, but our courts compel me to assault her physically and mentally even after such a brutal attack. Do you know how it feels to face a sweet young girl like Scooter after she has been raped and brutalized?"

Bill was angry. "I have to compound the nightmare she has just been through to collect evidence. Does anybody care? Does anybody really give a damn for the poor victim?" He clenched his fists and his knuckles whitened.

"Poor Scooter has been through hell and I have to welcome her back by submitting her to an internal examination. The courts tell me I have to take swabs just to check for semen because they won't believe her on the stand. I have to comb her pubic region in search of any hair left behind by the perpetrator, then I have to pluck a minimum of 20 hairs, preferably 50, according to the Rape Protocol Instructions, from her pubic region. I wish I could put a judge through that!

"Then, for her own health, I take blood samples and give her something for her pain. When I'm through with her, she looks at me like I am the rapist!"

"Evidence is necessary...." I began, but he interrupted me.

"Evidence is necessary so that you can arrest the suspect and we can force Scooter to relive this nightmare in court. Evidence is necessary so that the rapist can be set free because no one believed Scooter. Evidence is necessary so that even if we destroy poor Scooter on the witness stand, he will be eligible for parole in one third of his sentence. Free to rape again." Bill hung his head.

We both knew the truth. The animal that raped and brutalized poor Scooter probably already had been convicted for an identical crime. In all likelihood, he was out on an early work release program so that he could assimilate himself back into the community. Our combined experience in medicine and law enforcement taught us that violent sex-offenders were never successfully rehabilitated.

Never!

Our wise and compassionate judicial system, in its grand state of omniscience, fails to recognize that simple fact. As a result it continues to shove them out of prison, onto the streets — only to offend again.

"The system sucks," Bill said.

There was a silence in the room born out of desperation and fear. Desperation caused by our lack of ability to change the past and fear created from the possibility that we would never catch the animal that had savaged poor Scooter.

"Enough of this," Bev said. "We're feeling sorry for ourselves here while there is someone who needs us. Bob, we've got a job to do. Let's go see Scooter. Maybe we can get some details here that'll help us out. I know we're feeling sorry for Scooter but maybe if we can catch the bastard that raped her, we can put him away...."

"For a while?" I added.

Bev shook her head in agreement, stood up and walked out of the room. I followed.

For a moment, Bev and I stood outside the "Quiet Room," collecting our thoughts and formulating an interview strategy.

"Bev, we're gonna walk in there and ask some pretty painful questions. I hate this part. Poor Scooter's gonna have to relive this whole damn thing. She and her mother are going to hate us. We'll be lucky if they're even speaking to us after this interview."

"Yes, I know. Just follow my lead, Bobo. One of those cards you carry in your Deck taught me something I have used many times."

"What's that?"

"Sometimes ... Love is stronger than hate!"

Bev knocked softly on the door, below the sign which read QUIET ROOM.

"Come in," a woman's voice answered.

The room was dimly lit. Mrs. Fairchild sat on a two-seat sofa,

30

holding her daughter in her arms. A box of Kleenex, near-empty, was on the arm of the sofa and a waste paper basket held the used, clumped tissue.

"Mrs. Fairchild." Bev, who had gained the reputation of a gladiator amongst her fellow police officers, spoke with unusual quietness. "Could we talk for a while? There are a few questions I and my partner would like to ask Scooter. We'd like to catch the one who did this to her." Bev looked at Scooter's red face and swollen eyes. She was careful to include her in this conversation.

"What about it, Scooter? Feel like talking to the policemen?"

"Okay, Mom ... just...." She sniffed, then between sobs said, "...just please don't let me go."

Scooter was frightened. She withdrew almost to the point of leaving her mother's arms. In response, her mother moved with her, increasing the distance between us. Bev and I stood on one side of an invisible fence and they cowered on the other. I knew I could never hurdle such a fence alone. I did not have the skills that Bev had, so I watched as Bev worked her magic.

Although I was still as I observed Bev, inside, my stomach was twisting. Attempting to appear calm and serene while riding an emotional roller coaster is a skill most Police Officers strive to learn. They are like the proverbial duck swimming — calm and serene on the top, but peddling furiously below the surface.

My heart filled with anger and rage. If the scum-bag that had hurt Scooter had been within shooting distance....

"Scooter?" Bev knelt down. "Scooter? It's okay if I call you that isn't it?" Penny nodded. "Can we ask you a few questions? You don't have to answer if you don't want to, but we need your help, Scooter. We want to catch this man and put him in jail so he can never do this again."

Bev lied, but the lie was necessary if the first part of her promise was to be carried out. Both Bev and I knew that even if we succeeded in convicting the half-human who committed this crime on an innocent young child, he would be freed after serving less than half of his sentence. Bev lied about making the world a safer place, but her love and compassion for Scooter shone through and won her confidence. Bev had learned how to put aside her anger and hate and let compassion take over. It was a skill that was necessary at times like this. It was a skill that I had yet to master.

Scooter's face was red and tear swollen. Reaching out, Bev handed her a tissue while slowly and painstakingly pulling the details from her pain-clouded mind.

Scooter had been dropped off by her mother a short block away from the school. Her youthful pride insisted on her peers not

31

knowing that her mother had been her chauffeur. Today was a special day for Scooter. She planned to arrive two hours early where she and her classmates were to be admitted by the janitor so that they could decorate their classroom. It was their teacher's birthday and they had planned the surprise for two weeks. Ribbons were to be hung, balloons inflated, drawings pasted on the walls and a gift presented, formally, by a class of 15 young boys and girls.

A minute or so after watching her mother drive off, a large black car had pulled up. Scooter watched as the passenger's window was lowered almost magically as the driver sat erect in his seat. The man inside the car gripped the steering wheel as he told her he had just seen her mother involved in a car accident. Remembering what she had been taught in class and at home, Scooter began walking away from this suspicious car.

The man then exited his car and, as he limped over to her, described her mother's car. It was the accurate description of her mother's car that caught the young girl's attention. She aborted her escape. The suspect then took her by the arm, gently at first, then forcibly until he half-led, half-dragged her to the driver's door. Then he thrust her into the front seat.

"Can't use the passenger's door," he said. "Don't work." Scooter tried unsuccessfully to prove him a liar.

Carefully, Bev allowed Scooter to lead the conversation. We both filled several pages in our notebooks as she continued.

"Then he took me on a drive for about 10 minutes. I don't know where we went but I remember a long hill and then he parked the car on a narrow road or in a driveway. That's where he...." Scooter began to cry into the tissue that Bev held ready for this part of the interrogation.

"I'm gonna kill the bastard," Bev spoke so softly that only Scooter's Mother and I could hear.

Tears flowed freely in the Quiet Room. Between tears and tissues, a tale was told of the man who had raped and beaten young Scooter with a curved stick. She described how bad everything smelled.

"It was like our garbage can ... sort of ... but he smelled something like ... like...." she hesitated.

"What was it, Scooter?" her mother asked.

"Mom, remember when Dad lived with us?"

"Yes."

"Remember how bad his socks used to smell." Everyone laughed, including Scooter.

"Well, this man smelled like Dad's socks. His socks and our garbage can."

32

Penny continued to give her account of what had happened. Smells, sights, pain. She described it all. The interior of the car was dirty and filled with fast food-wrappers and small shiny boxes. There was a crack in the windshield, "shaped like a V," and everything was dirty and "sticky." Paper bags and the stale smell of food were foremost in her memory, but the presence of several "sticky boxes" were repeated during her narration. Scooter could not remember any printing on the boxes but they were "sort of silvery."

Flocks of sea gulls circling overhead, a bridge off in the distance — she even remembered how wet the dew had made the ground feel as the car ran over her. Scooter continued offering details that seemed unimportant but we listened and made notes. The assailant talked funny. "Sort of mumbles" she described his speech. "Like Dad when he used to drink — but he didn't smell like Dad did when he drank beer."

Scooter rambled on, describing the interior of the car as old and dirty but something made her think he had "painted" it. "It smelled like paint, or cleaning spray or something...." she added.

In 15 minutes the interview concluded and Bev turned her efforts to comforting Scooter and her mom.

"We'll catch that man," Bev promised. "You have my word." I could feel my jaw muscles clench as the pledge was given. We still had little evidence that would lead us to the suspect.

"Oh, one thing more," Bev added. "Scooter, that long mark on the side of your face. What caused it?"

"That's where he hit me with his stick."

"Can you describe the stick?"

"Yes. It's sort of like a bumpy stick with a hook on it. Kinda like the pictures in the Bible. Like the sticks that shepherds use."

"Like a walking stick?" Bev was careful not to suggest anything too specific.

"Like Gramma's stick," Scooter added.

"What kind of stick does Gramma have?" Bev asked Michelle.

"It's a cane. A bamboo cane."

"Yes, like Gramma's cane!" Scooter spoke out loud.

"Scooter," Bev added, "how long have you been wearing one earring?"

Her small hand reached up to her left ear and felt an earring. Feeling her other ear, she discovered that it was bare. "Oh, mom." She began to cry. "I've lost my butterfly!" The loss of her butterfly earring brought a cascade of tears. Scooter had just been savagely brutalized but the loss of her earring broke her spirit.

"My butterfly, Mom. I've lost my butterfly!"

Tears ran down her cheeks. Innocent tears, from an innocent soul.

We all watched as Scooter cried, each one of us in pain, each one of us wanting to take away hers.

Bev drew close to Scooter and hugged her. Scooter winced in anticipation of pain as she held her broken arm but Bev was gentle.

"Mrs. Fairchild," I spoke as we prepared to leave. "Bev has promised to catch the man that did this to your daughter. I'm not sure how we'll keep that promise, but it will happen."

I continued. "Scooter, your mom will keep you safe. Bev and I will drop in to your school to keep you and your friends safe. Don't worry, it'll never happen again. You got a cop's promise on that!" Scooter nodded.

"You going to call Pierre?" I asked Michelle. "I think her father should be advised.

"Yes. I'll call him. We were thinking of getting back together some day. Maybe this will...."

"Good." I filled in the silence. "Bev and I will call you later today. We'll let you know how things are. Is there anything we can do?"

"No, thanks."

"Okay. You take care, Scooter. Don't be surprised if you look out your window and see me or Bev cruisin' by. You're our special friend now and we'll keep an eye on you." I hoped this promise would help Scooter sleep better.

"Gee, thanks," she smiled.

"Oh, and one more thing, Scooter," I said.

"Yes?"

"I'll find your butterfly for you. I promise." Secretly I knew this promise might be impossible and I hoped that somewhere a jeweler would have a matching butterfly earring for sale.

I forced a smile as I turned to leave. " 'Bye Scooter. I'll see you later."

Bev and I walked out of the hospital. The sun had climbed into the sky and it felt warm. "You want to make the broadcast, or want me to do it?" Bev asked.

"You can do it. You got better notes," I confessed.

Two minutes later we sat in our cars and I keyed my microphone. "Surrey, Bravo 11 and 23 are 10-8."

"10-4," Sharon answered. "Any broadcast info?"

I looked over to Bev. She was busy reading her notes and preparing a brief history. In a few seconds she would condense our entire interview to a short 30-second broadcast. As I watched Bev, I admired her methodical approach. She was one of the best cops I had ever known.

But the pain came back.

34

And I cursed it.

I cursed the morning sun, the warm summer breeze and I cursed the son-of-a-bitch that would take away a young girl's innocence, virginity and butterfly earring. But amidst all the pain and fear, I would remember how Bev and I walked into a Quiet Room which was full of hurt, fear and resentment, yet through Bev's wisdom and love, brought two hurting souls into our lives. Somehow Bev had worked a miracle. She had taken in two strangers and, before we left the room, encircled them with her arms and heart.

Looking out of the driver's side window of my car, I saw Bev raise the microphone to her lips.

I admired Bev. She was a good soul.

CHAPTER 5

RUBBER CUP AND STICKY BOXES

"IMPOSSIBLE" ONLY DEFINES THE DEGREE OF DIFFICULTY.

Bev raised the mike to her lips as she held her notebook against the top of the steering wheel. Like most experienced Police Officers, she had mastered the "one-page thumb-flip." It was a one-handed technique used to hold open the notebook and turn the pages.

"Bravo 11, Surrey. Request priority this channel please for rape update." Bev asked for air-silence and warned all members on patrol that she was about to pass on information from our interview with Scooter.

"10-4 Bravo 11," Sharon acknowledged. Then she added, "Surrey all cars, stand-by for broadcast."

"Bravo 11, all cars." Bev's awareness now included only her notes and the microphone. "I have a BOLF and details regarding the rape of a young girl this morning. Standby one minute for details, please."

Bev took her thumb from the red microphone button and checked her watch. One minute would give ample warning for all Police Officers to pull over and ready their notebooks. All Police Officers, that is, except Stewart Dudzinski. He had a reputation for stopping his police car in preparation for any broadcast, no matter how routine the broadcast or where he was at that particular moment.

Dudzinski would sit at a stoplight while it cycled red, green, amber, then red again while he took notes. Later, when a complaint from the public was received and he was called into the Sergeant's office, he would defend his actions. "There's lotsa room, they can go around me. When somebody makes a broadcast I give it priority." Dudzinski was the finest cop I had ever met. His fondness for chewing tobacco, karate and small animals made him somewhat of an enigma, but his prowess as an investigator was without match. He had a mind like a filing cabinet and a notebook filled with hand-

36

writing only he could read. Clearly, his intellect surpassed his penmanship. Stewart had passed up many opportunities for promotion and was not well liked by upper management. He did not fit into their mold. He did, however, fit into the mold of "street-cop." He would eventually accept a promotion to detective where his investigative skills would be put to good use.

For now, however, Stewart was content merely to solve the crimes that occurred when he was on duty, leaving the complicated investigations to the "sleuths with the three-piece suits and tiny guns." Stewart often referred to detectives as being over-dressed and under-armed.

"Bravo 11, all cars, stand-by for broadcast." Bev gave a final warning. Five seconds later she announced: "Bravo 11, all cars, I have an update on the rape which occurred in Zone 2 this morning. The victim is a young girl age 13 years. Name Penny Allison Fairchild — I spell surname, F.A.I.R.C.H.I.L.D.. While on her way to school this morning, she was abducted by an unknown adult male who drove her to an unidentified location where he repeatedly beat and raped her. Stop check." Bev released the microphone to allow enough time for notes to be made, opinions to be offered and the lump in her throat to clear. "Continuing ... vehicle description is as follows: Large, dark, possibly black vehicle likely equipped with electric windows. V-shaped crack in the windshield. Front passenger door does not open from the inside. Interior of vehicle littered with fast-food containers and wrappers and described only as dirty and sticky. Vehicle may contain a bamboo cane, or similar type stick. Victim has lost one small butterfly-type earring which may still be in car.

"Location of incident not known but victim described smell of garbage cans in area.

"Suspect described as adult male. No accent or physical deformities or other descriptors except for the mention of a limp. In addition, the victim stated that she thought he smelled like old socks. Stop check."

Silence.

"Continuing ... victim was beaten and raped several times...." Bev's voice showed emotion. "I repeat, beaten and raped several times. She's 13 years old, guys. We need a major BOLF on this one." Then her face regained its composure. "Any info please update Bravo 11." Bev added one last plea. "This is a bad one, guys, I need your help this time, please?"

"Bravo 11?" Sharon's voice came over the dispatch channel.

"Bravo 11," Bev answered.

"I have all the info necessary. I'll fan it out on C.P.I.C. to all

37

Lower Mainland Detachments and P.D.'s." Sharon had promised to pass this information through our Canadian Police Information Center to every dispatcher in the Lower Mainland. She would title the message: URGENT — FOR IMMEDIATE BROADCAST TO ALL CARS, then add as a personal touch, PLEASE! Sharon had previously been admonished for putting Please on the computer fan-out network. The word was not officially sanctioned.

Sharon did not care about policy.

"Thanks, Sharon. Bravo 11 and 23 clear from S.M.H."

"10-4, clear of Surrey Memorial Hospital," Sharon confirmed, then added, "Any word on Higgy?"

"No change," I advised.

"10-4."

I backed out of my parking stall then drove up tight to Bev's car. "Nice broadcast, Bev, but how'd you know about the electric windows?"

"Don't you remember Scooter describing how the passenger's window was lowered? She said it was like magic? The suspect didn't lean over. She even remembered seeing both his hands on the wheel. Obviously, he had electric windows." Since Bev had even included the sticky interior of the vehicle, I allowed her this one extrapolation of the facts without question.

"Bravo 11, Bravo 6," Dudzinski called Bev.

"Bravo 6," she answered.

"You sure about that smell?"

"The socks?" Bev confirmed. "According to Scooter uh ... the victim ... yes. He smelled like her father's socks."

"That's all I wanted to know."

"Why? You got a suspect, Stu?" Bev asked.

"Make a meet?" He had asked to meet her in person. "How about the Flats, the Cancer Dump," he suggested.

"Five minutes. I'll be there." Bev replied.

Stewart had suggested a location near the banks of the Fraser River where the previous week we had discovered several large electrical transformers. They were old and seeping an oily liquid. "Probably PCB's. Touch this stuff and you get to be a Cancer-Mutant," Stu said when we had looked at the leaky metal casings.

"Coming, Bob?" Bev called out as she drove away.

I shoved my car into gear and followed her to the flats. If anyone could solve this crime, it would be Stewart Dudzinski.

Heading north on King George Highway, I wondered what plan Stewart had in mind. Why the flats? It was the oldest area in Surrey, populated with run-down, small wooden houses and occupied by a mixture of welfare recipients and bikers. Certainly

38

Dudzinski had a plan. Just as certainly, I did not know what it was.

A few minutes later Bev and I arrived at the pre-arranged location. Pulling over to the side of the road, I clipped a portable radio to my gunbelt and exited my police car.

"Hey, Dudz! Watchya got?" I called to Stewart who was sitting on the hood of his car, staring at several leaking electrical transformers a short distance from the road.

Stewart did not return my greeting.

Bev was walking in our direction. Briefly our eyes met and we both pondered the same question. "Why here? What does Dudzinski have planned?"

The gravel crunched under our feet as we walked in single file alongside the road. Stopping a few feet from Dudzinski's front bumper, we watched as he sat motionless, staring at the leaky, oil-coated metal casings.

Then he turned and with one finger of his right hand, motioned us closer. Turning toward Bev, he spoke, "Tell me more about this bastard."

"You've got everything that I have. I gave it all over the radio," she answered.

"No. There's more. Talk to me, Bev. Tell me about the interview. Tell me everything."

Stewart was a master interrogator and could harvest the most minute details from anyone. Bev reviewed the interview, referring to her notes. In three minutes she had delivered the entire contents of the interview. Dudzinski made no notes. He just listened.

Reading from her notes, Bev described the filth and rubbish inside the vehicle. She also described how Scooter remembered the area. The smell of garbage, socks, how "sticky" everything seemed inside the car.

"Tell me more about the smells. Kids remember how things feel and smell more than how they look." Bev reviewed the recollection of the smell of paint.

"Paint?" Stewart's eyes opened wide. "Paint?"

"Paint or cleaning fluid," Bev added, reading from her notes.

"Paint? Sticky? Socks? Describe the garbage in the car." Stewart was now fully involved in Scooter's memories. He was smelling what Scooter smelled and feeling what she had felt.

"Fast-food wrappers, a few small cardboard or foil boxes — sticky boxes she called them — a couple of...."

"Small boxes?" Stewart interrupted.

"Uh, yes, that's what I've got in my notes."

"That's enough." He smiled. "I know the bastard. I know him dammit. I know him."

"Why did you want to meet us here?" Bev asked.

"See that ooze? See all the carcinogens?" He pointed to the transformers. "I'm gonna wipe his face in that before the end of our shift."

"How?" Bev asked. "Who are we looking for? What are you thinking, Dudz?"

"See that?" Stewart pointed to the Port Mann Bridge in the distance. It was barely visible. "You go back and ask Scooter if she could see the bridge."

"No need to do that. She told me there was a bridge but it was a fair distance away."

"That's all I need to know."

Dudzinski slid from the hood of his car, turned and reached in for the microphone.

"Bravo 6, Surrey," he called.

"Bravo 6," Sharon answered.

"Speak to the Sarge, please?"

Stewart pulled a face and looked skyward as he waited.

"Bravo 6, go ahead!" Sergeant Denis called.

"Sarge, I'd like to be coded 10-6 for the remainder of the shift if you don't mind. Got a few enquires to make on the rape that took place this morning." Dudzinski's 10-6 request meant that he was "Busy — excluded from calls" so that he could follow his feelings and possibly help solve the rape.

"Negative! We're under-manned as it is. Stay on the air."

"10-4. I agree. That's fair. Thanks Sarge." Stewart used his talents at making rhymes to convert "Stay on the air" to "That's fair." Sergeant Denis was not amused.

"Do you copy me, Dudzinski?" the Sarge's voice clearly came over the radio. "Do you copy me? I said stay on...." Squelch — whistle — garble.

Bev had keyed the microphone on her portable, causing interference and turning Denis' voice into a combination of squelches, whistles and fragmented words.

"Sorry, Sarge," Dudzinski called back. "Reception is really bad down here on the Flats. Thanks for agreeing, though." Then he turned the volume down on his police radio.

"Y'all heard the man. He just gave me permission." Stewart winked and smiled. "You did hear him — didn't you?"

"Absolutely, no question about it, clear as a bell!" Bev and I nearly sang our agreements together.

"Sure wish we had better radio reception down here." Bev

40

made an entry into her notebook, complaining of the poor radio reception.

"Any other questions why we made the meet here?" Dudzinski's mouth turned up at the corners. We both understood that an excuse of poor radio reception would be Stewart's alibi in the event that Sergeant Denis would not give him permission to dedicate the day in search of Scooter's rapist.

"Hey, Dudz," Bev called as he turned to climb into his car. "Make it so! Please? Bring the bastard in."

Dudzinski slammed his car door. As he pulled onto the asphalt I heard him say, "This one's for Scooter."

Bev and I watched as Bravo 6 drove away, leaving behind only a small dusty trail and a promise.

"Think he knows what he's doing?" Bev asked.

"Ya. He'll find that pervert. He's a master! Best cop I've ever known and...." I paused for a moment.

"And?" Bev brought my thoughts back to the present.

"...and last week he asked to photocopy one of the cards in my Deck. The one which says:

> ### To fail is not a crime —
> ### To stop trying is!

"That's Stewart for sure." Bev looked down the road that Dudzinski had just driven. "Hey, get that Deck out — let's see what we should do next."

"Think it'll help?" I questioned her decision.

"You always said it was magic and that is just what we need. C'mon Bobo, out with it?"

I reached into the breast pocket of my patrol jacket and retrieved the Deck. Removing the cloth, I handed it to Bev. "Your idea. Your cut."

"Let's see now if I got this right. Shuffle. Cut. Turn over the top card."

Bev followed the same ritual I had set for myself years ago. She read the top card out loud:

> ### The wise man listens
> ### while all others speak.

"Okay, how does that help us?"

"It's a shame this Deck was wasted on you. Dudz found clues in my notes I made from Scooter's description. Let's review them."

After 10 minutes of dissecting our notes we were no further ahead.

"The area where this happened smelled like garbage and it

was about a 10-minute drive from Scooter's summer school. There was a long hill." Bev verbally summarized all the evidence.

"That's here! The Flats! By God, Dudzinski is onto something," I said.

"Except the bridge. Can't see any bridge from here," Bev countered.

"What about the Patullo Bridge?"

"Too far, that would be at least 20 minutes from the school."

"The Port Mann?"

"My God, that's it. The Port Mann Bridge. Straight north of the school, down Grosvenor Road and even...."

"That hairpin turn!" I added.

"But that would put us...."

"At the entrance to the municipal dump." I completed her sentence.

"Garbage! Beautiful garbage and a perfect view of the Port Mann Bridge! Yes!"

Five minutes later we had parked our cars at the main road leading to the municipal dump. Standing beside our police cars we surveyed the scene. "It's perfect. Smells just right. There's the Port Mann Bridge and look...." Bev pointed toward the sky.

The sky was dotted with sea gulls. Feathered rats. They had been arriving at the dump since before dawn for their day's feast on old meat, maggots and other wondrous morsels.

"So far so good. We got smell, sea gulls and a bridge, but this road is too wide," I said.

"Ha! Follow me." Bev slipped back into her car and spun gravel from under her wheels as she sped down the road. Three hundred yards later she turned right and disappeared. Following her, I turned into a short gravel road which ended a mere 50 feet from the paved road. Bev had stopped her car just as she entered the short by-way. She was already standing, waving to me to follow as I pulled up.

"If this is the scene of the crime, we'd better walk lightly," she said.

Over the next half hour we systematically scoured every square inch of the gravel road and the bushes which had grown thick since spring.

Nothing. No fast-food wrappers, no earring, nothing. The course surface of the gravel road did not even allow tire marks.

Just as we had decided to leave, Bev pointed to the edge of the road. "What's that?"

I walked in the direction her finger pointed.

"No! Freeze! Don't touch it!" Walking past me she knelt down. I squatted beside her.

42

"What is it?" I asked.

"Don't know." Bev's eyes studied a small brown rubber cup. It was a small vessel about the size of a whiskey-shot glass, worn on the bottom and dirty.

"It's just garbage," I suggested.

"No." She pointed to the bushes nearby and the ground surrounding the rubber cup. "See the leaves, the gravel and everything around us."

"Ya."

"What do you see?"

"Leaves, gravel, dirt."

"No! Wet leaves. Wet gravel. Wet dirt. We had a heavy dew last night. Everything here is wet."

"So what?" I asked.

"The cup is dry! Don't touch it. I'll be right back."

A minute later she returned from her car with an exhibit bag. Carefully, she picked up the cup, placed it in the bag, peeled the paper strip from the top of the clear plastic bag and pressed the adhesive ribbon over the top. Taking a pen from her shirt pocket, she signed her name to it, along with the date and time. Without speaking, she made an entry in her notebook, confirming the circumstances surrounding her discovery.

"Think it's important?" I asked.

"Ask Scooter," Bev replied as she placed the exhibit bag into her trunk and slammed the lid.

"Remember that Deck of yours?" she said.

"Yes."

"There's a card in it that says:

***Anything we do may be unimportant,
but it is important that we do it anyway.***

"I'd rather have a trunk full of garbage than miss one clue that might put that pervert behind bars."

Bev was precise in all that she did. I knew better than to doubt or ever question her motives. "Let's go. I owe you a breakfast," she said.

We drove away from the landfill site, both hoping the suspect drank from a small, dirty rubber cup approximately one inch in diameter and two inches high. We didn't know it but that small rubber cup would bring a surprise later in the day.

CHAPTER 6

IT'S ALIVE!

IT IS OFTEN WISE TO JUDGE A BOOK BY ITS COVER.
GARBAGE RARELY COMES ATTRACTIVELY PACKAGED.

Leaving the suspected scene of the crime felt good. Only time would tell whether or not the small rubber cup would be a valuable piece of evidence and even though it seemed unlikely, at least we had done something.

One of the worst feelings a Police Officer experiences is helplessness. Police Officers chose their profession because they want to help. When a situation rendered any cop powerless, incapable of providing assistance, a deep feeling of failure was the result.

The slight chance that we had discovered the crime scene and seized evidence felt uplifting. As I drove away from the small gravel road, I glanced in my rear view mirror and mentally reaffirmed my promise to find the inhuman pervert who hurt Scooter.

The sun was shining and I could feel its warmth on my arm as I drove up Grosvenor Road. It was well past breakfast time but I was not hungry. Anger and fear are great appetite suppressants. Still, breakfast was a ritual meeting that was overdue, as I was about to be reminded.

"Bravo 16, Bravo 11," Bev was calling Rod, our Corporal and one of the finest supervisors a cop could ask for.

"Bravo 11," he acknowledged.

"Breakfast at Bino's?" Bev asked.

"Who's goin'?" Rod always picked his company carefully. Normally he would eat breakfast or drink coffee with anyone, but there were a few snitches on the Watch who took great delight in reporting to the Sarge.

"Just me and the worm," Bev replied, knowing that my little-used nickname would annoy me just enough to displace the memory of Scooter for an instant.

"Be there in five minutes. Room for a rookie?" Rod asked.

"Always!"

Rod had been recently promoted, and with his promotion he promised us all that he would never forget the fact that "A

44

Constable is merely a support system designed to do all the work and make the Corporals look good."

Rod was unlike any other Corporal. He was never afraid to get dirty, to arrest the filthiest of drunks or to face the most dangerous of situations. He worked night shift alongside all of the Constables and was usually the first through the door at a family fight, drug raid or prowler call. In spite of that, he never wore a bullet-proof vest under his uniform shirt.

Rod was "old-school." He was set in his ways, the kind of cop that I would want to appear if I ever needed help. He was street-wise, compassionate and honest.

I followed Bev's car into the parking lot. We walked into the restaurant and found a table. Moments later Rod and his new recruit joined us.

"Good morning, officers," Rod said, pretending to be formal. "May I have the honor of introducing you to Constable Smelly." The recruit's face turned red. "Yes, just one day with ol' Smelly and I'm already wanting to kick him out of the car."

"Smelly?" Bev asked, ignoring the young man who stood red-faced beside Rod.

"Smelly!" Rod sat down. "We were only five minutes into the shift and he steps in doggy-do. To make matters worse, he then tracks it inside my car and smushes it all over the floor and the firewall."

"How do you do, Smelly?" Bev offered her hand in friendship.

"Fine thanks," he blushed and shook her hand.

"Name's Bev. This is Bob," she said." And you have our apologies for having to ride with Corporal Big Mouth."

A strange silence descended upon us as our eyes watched our new friend. He was fresh from the Academy and had not yet learned how to behave. His Corporal had just been insulted and he felt awkward.

"That's okay, buddy," Rod explained. "They call me big mouth because I'm the only one on the Watch who can hold a billiard ball in his mouth.

Smelly just grinned and said, "Really?"

"What will you have?" A cheery waitress greeted our table.

"Spanish omelettes all around." Rod announced. "We're celebrating and I'm buying. It's a long story but it involves a siren and a spilled cup of coffee."

"Hey," Rod continued, "did you guys hear Denis at briefing?" He sat tall and stiff in his chair as he mocked the Sergeant. "The executive washroom is now off limits to the rank and file members. I don't suppose anyone here knows why?"

45

Bev and I collapsed in laughter, then regained our composure as we looked at Rod's new recruit. Several members of our watch were responsible for the new restrictions on the use of the executive washroom.

"Well, yes," Bev said. "Did you hear the rumor that a roving gang of Constables raided the executive washroom in our Detachment Commander's office last Saturday morning?"

"No," the recruit admitted.

"Well, it seems last week that after a marauding band of Constables had partaken in breakfast at Bino's they all used the Big Man's washroom. All of them."

"So?" he asked.

"Well, it seems they all forgot to flush the executive toilet. When the Big Man entered his office Monday morning, well, I guess he got what he deserved."

"How so?"

"Someone had left a sign on his door, typed on his own typewriter. It said 'You dump on us. We dump on you!'"

"So what's the big deal?" the recruit asked.

"Well, I guess it kinda got high and hard over the hot summer weekend and they had to call a plumber in from the Municipal Hall."

"Excuse me, but how do you know so much about it?" Smelly asked.

"Oh, just rumor. The word gets around." Bev's smile left her face as she added, "Information goes only one way on this Watch. Understand, my friend? One way. No one snitches to the boss. No one. Understand young man? No one!" Bev made it very clear to her new brother that there was a closeness, a brotherhood, a trust amongst Police Officers that was not to be broken.

"Until the day comes when Denis decides to come out from behind his desk and get dirty, he'll never be one of us. How long you been with Rod?"

"Just a couple of days. They tell me my trainer will be picked very soon and...."

"I'm trying to assign Dudzinski to him," Rod interrupted.

"You should be so lucky." Bev looked at the young face and smiled. "What's your real name?"

"Smelly," Rod jumped in.

"Shut up, Rod. Your name?" Bev turned toward Smelly.

"It's Francis. Francis Pinkewycz."

"Smelly," Rod again offered.

"Ain't no one gonna survive with a name like Francis Pinky Whizz. We'll call you Frank," Bev suggested.

46

"Okay," Frank agreed.

Bev looked directly at Rod while she spoke. She did not like the nickname Smelly and Rod conceded. Smelly no longer existed. His name would be Frank.

"Now, before anyone gets hold of you and screws with your brains, let me tell you something about being a cop. Here's how it goes. I'll walk through Hell to save your butt and you'll walk through Hell to save mine. Ain't none of us ever alone no matter how bad it hurts, or why. We're a family. You can call me Sis if you like and I can call you Frank, but when the chips are down we're all we got and you will never never back down if we need help."

Bev sipped at her coffee. The conversation had turned serious. "See Teather here? He slurs his speech when he gets tired. Know why? Don't answer, I'll tell you. Because some lame-brained, spineless SOB screwed off in the opposite direction when he called in a 10-33. He was left alone. They kicked the shit out of him just like Crazy Fred kicked the shit out of Higgy yesterday."

Bev reached across the table and placed her hand on the new recruit's and lowered her voice. "Know what a 10-33 is?"

He shook his head.

"It means 'I'm on the ground, fading fast and getting the shit kicked out of me.' When you hear a 10-33 you will come running, ready to wade through hell and dance with the Devil if necessary." Then, in a very quiet voice, she added, "Have I made this clear enough?"

"Yes, ma'am."

"Welcome aboard, Brother. In this line of work you always get the tests first and the lessons later, but hang around and we'll have some fun. Heck we'll even show you...."

"Excuse me." The waitress sat our plates on the table and filled our coffee cups. The table went silent except for the clinks of cheap knives and forks on porcelain.

I looked at my plate. Red-specked Spanish omelette, side order of hash-browns, two strips of bacon and a sprig of parsley. I wasn't hungry.

"Earth calling, Bobo?" Rod asked. "Not eating today?"

"Ya, sure ... I'm...." I pushed the plate aside.

"Look at that man, Frank. Take a long hard look. You wanna be just like him some day. He's learned to care." Rod's partner nodded.

"Look, Bob," Rod paused, then said, "Scooter's got you by the shorts, hasn't she?" I nodded. "Hey, you got Dudzinski on the case. I heard him pretending he couldn't hear Denis on the air. I bet he's out right now tracking the son-of-a-bitch down."

"Okay," I agreed.

47

I sipped at my coffee and looked back at Rod. He knew how I felt. He was trying to help but everyone at the table knew there wasn't anything that could make me feel better.

"Look, Rod," I said. "Higgy gets bumped and Scooter gets raped. It's only three hours into the shift and I've had enough. I'm okay. Just back off a bit, will ya'?"

"Okay, Bob." Rod understood. "I'll even eat your omelette for you."

"Don't let this worry you, Frank," Bev said over a mouthful of egg. "Hang around long enough and you'll learn what this job is really all about. Maybe sooner than you'd expect."

"Yes, Ma'am," Frank replied.

"No Ma'am here. It's Bev, Sis or, if you like...."

"Cannibal." I completed her sentence. "Y'know, Frank, some day we'll tell you about the time she bit off half of a biker's ear."

"Not just any biker." Bev sat straight and tall.

"Ya, you're right, Sis. Not just any biker. It was Wiener. Sergeant-at-Arms of our local chapter of Hells Angels." I sipped my coffee. "It's a long story." I looked at Bev and winked. "We'll tell you about it some day. Who knows, if Rod manages to buddy you up with Dudzinski, you'll have your own stories to tell. Why in about...."

"Ksshhht, Bravo 6, Surrey," Rod's portable called out. Rod reached to his gunbelt and unholstered his portable radio.

"Bravo 6 on portable."

"Bravo 6 how do you copy?"

"Five by Three," Rod answered. We always rated our reception on a scale of one to five, with one being totally unacceptable and five being perfect. Rod's answer told Sharon that he received her signal very loud but not very clear. Five by Five meant "loud and clear."

"Bravo 6 I have a priority for you and Constable Pinkewycz. Ready to copy?" Rod already had his notebook open on the table.

"We have a report of a D.B. in the bushes on the north side of the Flamingo Hotel parking lot."

"Copy," Rod confirmed the message. A D.B. meant a dead body — presumably human. "You got E.H.S. on the way?" He had asked if Emergency Health Services had been dispatched.

"10-4. Already dispatched," Sharon confirmed.

"We'll be there in three." Rod holstered his radio. "C'mon Frank — you're about to lose your virginity. Ever seen a dead body before?" Frank shook his head. "Well, five bucks says you don't keep your omelette down."

"We'll cover you, Rod," I said as we all stood up. "Kinda

48

brings back memories doesn't it, Sis?" Bev nodded. She was remembering her first sudden death. We had attended it together. It was a hanging. A suicide. Bev had been assigned to cut down the body and log the exhibits.

"Just like the ol' days," she said.

Rod pulled out $12 and left it on the table. Normally, the police were never charged for meals they did not finish. If our duties called us away before finishing our meal there was no charge. Bino's was good to us, however, and only charged half price when we had the time to eat our entire meal so we never squelched on the bill. We always paid for the meal and left a healthy tip for the waitress, whether or not we finished.

A few minutes later our cars squealed to a halt on the parking lot which served the Flamingo Beer Parlor. Rod and Frank were out of their car ahead of Bev and me and already looking into the bush.

"Whatcha got, Rod?" I called as we walked up behind them.

"Sweet Mother of God," Rod called back. "It's Scabby!"

Scabby was a local glue-sniffer. He had lived to the ripe old age of 35, although most of his years were spent either in jail or in a solvent-induced haze. Scabby was known to nearly everyone. When his welfare cheque was late and he could not afford a good quality airplane glue, he stopped at a self-serve gas station and purchased five cents worth of high octane. Just enough to wet a rag. Scabby had taste, though. He always ordered unleaded gasoline, proclaiming it was better for his health.

After throwing a nickel in through the window, he would stumble away, holding his octane-enriched handkerchief tight to his face. Usually his departure was staggered and he would curl up on the sidewalk within a block of the gas station. He had earned the name Scabby because of the gashes, cuts and scrapes on his face which never had time to heal before more were inflicted by an uncaring sidewalk. Scabby's face looked like it had caught fire and someone had tried to put it out with an axe.

"Holy Baldy," Bev called out, "Ol' Scabby's died and gone to Acetone Heaven." We all stood looking at the back of a body which had been abused by alcohol, drugs and glue.

Rod administered the first exam to his new recruit. "Well, young man, he's face down and stiff. Wanna roll him over. Don't worry, he's lying in clean sand. He won't hurt you."

Frank approached Scabby cautiously at first, then, sensing our thrill at his timidness, he stepped lively, leaned forward and rolled the corpse over."

"Sweet Mother of God!" Rod repeated his favorite expres-

49

sion. "Just look at him — he's got a face like a breaded veal cutlet!" We all laughed. Few people will ever understand why Police Officers laugh at death. Perhaps it is because we see so much of it we become calloused. Perhaps it is fear. Perhaps it is because we have shed too many tears and now our cries, being tearless, just sound like laughter.

"Well, my young friend," Rod ordered, "don't stop there. Sure he's cold and stiff but is he dead? C'mon, young feller, check for a carotid pulse. Check for breathing. Is he bleeding? Any bullet wounds? Any knives sticking out of him. C'mon man, you wanted to be a cop. Hop to it!"

The young recruit leaned forward and laid his fingers gently on the side of Scabby's trachea. "I ... I think there's something ... I ... oh my God! Shit!" Pinkewycz jumped back as Scabby opened his eyes and let out a hissing sound.

"It's alive!" Frank screamed. "Oh my God, it's alive!"

"Scabby, you're still with us!" Bev called. "Great. That means we don't have to do all the paperwork."

"Okay, who's gonna give him a ride back to the Handcuff Hilton?" I asked, looking at the remnants of a man who smelled worse than the bottom of Frank's shoes.

"Frank," Rod ordered, "load him up. We'll take him back to the Crowbar Hotel and, who knows, maybe check him into the Bridal Suite." Rod often referred to the Drunk Tank as the "Bridal Suite" for reasons only he understood. "Help the poor struggler, Frank. I'll open the rear door."

Rod walked 20 feet to his police car and swung the door open wide. Bev and I wanted to help Frank but this was not the time. He had to show us he was not afraid. He had to demonstrate his desire to be "one of the family."

He had to prove himself worthy. And he did.

In one move, Constable Pinkewycz swung old Scabby over his shoulders and walked towards Rod. Stopping at the rear door, he muttered, "Watch your head, Scabby," then unceremoniously dumped the half-dead hulk onto the rear seat.

"Well done, buddy! You're gonna be okay." Rod complimented the grace and strength shown by his new recruit. Deep down, however, he was really complimenting Frank for his courage. It is not an easy first-time task to pick up a half-dead drunk so diseased that flakes of skin fell like snow over Frank's patrol jacket as he carried him to the waiting car.

"Well done, buddy." Rod patted him on the shoulder, then turned to us and winked. "Just when you think you've won the rat race, along comes a faster rat." Rod was referring to Frank. He had suspected that his new recruit would back down. But he did not.

"Looks like the Academy is turning out some high-class recruits for a change," Bev said.

"No." Frank looked at us as he brushed the flakes of skin from his patrol jacket. "No, as a matter of fact they tell us not to touch something like that." He pointed towards the rear seat of Rod's car. "They tell us to leave it for the Paramedics."

"So why didn't you leave him?" Rod asked.

"'Cause you asked me to put him in the car." Frank answered Rod's question with a simple sentence.

"Frank, you and I are gonna get along just great!" Rod threw his arm over his young recruit's shoulders and grinned. "C'mon, buddy." Rod handed him the car keys. "You can drive the Buffalo Cab. Let's go back to the barn."

We often referred to our police cars as the "Buffalo Cabs" because of the crest on the white door — the letters RCMP, and a prominent figure of a buffalo's head.

"Wow," Bev said, "Rod's letting someone else drive his police car. Well, I'll never...."

"Neither will I...."

"Think we ought to...."

"Follow them back?" I finished her sentence. Mental telepathy was common among Police Officers who worked together. "Let's see how ol' Smelly performs in the cell block."

Bev smiled, then added. "I ain't never seen Scabby skin-searched before. Should be a hoot!"

Frank had already impressed Rod. Heck, he had impressed us. Now we would see how he conducted himself under even more adverse conditions.

Although the ride to the cells was only 10 minutes, the memories of the morning returned — Scooter. Higgy. A block from the police station I picked up my microphone and called.

"Bravo 23, Bravo 16." I wanted to talk to Stu. Hopefully he was hot on a trail and could give us some good news.

"Bravo 23, Bravo 16," I called again.

"Bravo 23, it seems Dudzinski is having trouble with his radio. Do you want an alternate?"

"No thanks, Sharon. Got it. Mark me and Bev 10-7 the office, please." Stewart carried a cellular telephone in his briefcase. I would call him after we had booked in Scabby.

"Surrey, Bravo 16, open the bay door please." Rod called in, stating he was waiting to drive his police car into the secure parking. Once inside, the large steel overhead door closed. He and Frank would exit the vehicle, lock their sidearms into secure alu-

51

minum boxes, tuck the keys into their pockets, then allow their prisoner freedom.

It was a limited freedom, though. With the overhead door closed securely there was only one exit and the door to the booking-in room stood ajar.

Rod and Frank walked Scabby into the booking area and allowed him to sit on the floor. Bev and I entered through the office door and stood behind the counter to witness our new friend's "rite of passage."

"He's all yours, Frank. Seize him and search him, cuff him and stuff him. By time you're through I want to know how many dirty tissues are in his pockets, how much money he has on him, the color of his underwear and his shoe size."

Pinkewycz looked pale.

"Okay, Corp. Yassir, Mass'r." He spoke in a southern slave accent. "Scabby, you got any needles in your pockets?"

"No, sir," Scabby muttered.

"You got any identification?" Scabby pulled a brown envelope from his pocket and handed it to Frank. "C'mon, Rod," Frank pleaded. "It's got snot on it. Do I really....?"

"Here." Rod tossed his friend a pair of disposable rubber gloves.

"Thanks, bud." Frank disappeared briefly around the corner then returned with a large floor fan. Turning it on, he directed it toward Scabby. "There ya' go. Now you stay down wind and we won't have any problems, will we."

In the next five minutes Francis reported that Scabby had 11 cents, brown underwear and three dirty tissues.

"Aren't you forgetting something?" Rod asked. "His shoe size. Take 'em off and tell me his shoe size."

What Constable Pinkewycz was to experience was not covered in any Police Officer's handbook, nor was it ever addressed in any lecture at the Police Academy. Scabby wore three pairs of socks. The first pair came off easily and although they had a stiffness about them, they were definitely socks.

The second pair came off with great difficulty and made a sound like Velcro being separated.

The third pair brought a smile to Rod and a look of panic to Frank.

"What ... they're ... uh, Rod I ... How do you...." Frank Pinkewycz was speechless. Scabby never changed socks. When his socks became too thin he merely went dumpster diving until he found a new pair and placed them over the old ones. Frank was looking at something few people had ever seen.

52

Scabby's toenails and skin had grown through the weave of several layers of cotton, wool and polyester. At least three layers of cloth were still wrapped around his ankles but the bottom portions had all grown together. The only way Scabby's socks could ever be removed would be under the deft hand of a surgeon.

"Aw...." Frank gagged and turned away.

"Yup," Rod said. "Kinda knocks a guy off his food, doesn't it. Hey, Frank, ever realize just how similar the smell of old socks is to hot buttered popcorn?"

Francis Pinkewycz never ate popcorn again.

"You're not through. Check his identification from his welfare cheque stub, fill in the Prisoner's Log and take him to his room." Rod ensured proper procedure would be followed.

Five minutes later, Scabby was given a cell of his own. Frank felt sorry for the poor man and his flesh-eating socks and decided the drunk tank would be too inhumane.

"Want me to run him?" Pinkewycz asked. Policy dictated that all prisoners have their name queried on the Canadian Police Information Center computers immediately after booking in.

"Naw. His name is Lyle Houseman and he's been a steady customer at this fine establishment for the past five years. Houseman has a record as long as your arm. In his younger years he was a safe cracker, then as glue took over his brains, he deteriorated to armed robbery, theft, and shoplifting. I think he got picked up on a sexual assault charge once but the courts ruled him crazy. Spent a year in Thornton Valley Home for the Criminally Insane but they let him go. Just mark the C.P.I.C. box as checked and we'll let him sleep it off. He's a pretty good prisoner. Doesn't talk much and hardly ever screams."

Bev turned to me and smiled. "I guess they've changed their teaching at the Academy, hey Bobo. It's been years since we've had a recruit like this one."

"Ya, years...." My mind drifted back 15 years. Back to Regina, Saskatchewan, back to basic training ... back to Physical Education ... back to hell:

"Okay, you dozy little men. When I say run I mean run." Our Physical Education instructor positioned himself in front of us. We all stood at attention. As he moved up and down the front line, spit from his mouth flew out in an arc, missing some of us and landing on the unlucky ones. "When I say run, you will run until you drop. When I say stand up and keep running you will do just that. Only when you pass out in your own vomit will you be allowed the luxury of rest. But don't think you'll escape me then 'cause when you wake up I've a special treat for you."

53

Corporal Brinell was about to teach us a very important lesson and it had nothing to do with running. "Now run!"

He pointed toward the far corner of the gymnasium and 32 recruits began to run in a clockwise direction around the walls of hell.

We ran until our legs became numb and our lungs burned. We ran until the sweat rolled into our eyes and we were half-blind. We ran until we could think of nothing but the pain. We ran until the first man dropped. This time it was Fogarty.

"Attennnshuuun!" Brinell screamed and we all halted. Thirty-one recruits, red-faced, sweating and slobbering, stood at attention. Nothing moved but our chests as they heaved up and down uncontrollably. Brinell walked over to Fogarty's unconscious body.

"Whatsamatter you funny little dweeb?" Brinell shouted, then reached down and dragged Fogarty to the center of the gymnasium. Twice he kicked the near-lifeless body. Fogarty twitched, rolled over onto his back then opened his eyes. Brinell placed his foot on Fogarty's abdomen then pushed down.

Fogarty vomited. He blew chunks until he was purple. Gagging, retching and crying he emptied his lunch onto the freshly waxed gym floor. When he had quit vomiting, he sat up, leaned on one arm and wiped his mouth.

"Clean it up you dizzy little man," Brinell ordered. "NOW!" he screamed.

Fogarty stood up and wobbled, then he began to walk toward the two swinging doors. He was going for a bucket and mop.

"I never gave you permission to leave this room did I?" Brinell screamed.

"No, Corporal," a weak Fogarty admitted.

"Then you get your butt back here and clean up this mess. If you don't I'll mop it up with your lifeless body!" Fogarty walked back to the pudding he had left on the floor. "Scoop up that mess with your hands. Can't be much more than a cup or two." Fogarty knelt and complied with the order. "Now wipe it on your singlet." Fogarty wiped the mess onto his chest. "Now, all of you will take off your singlets and wipe up the liquid until this floor shines!" In turn, 31 recruits removed their cotton singlets and swept them over the floor where Fogarty had left his lunch.

There were many such rituals in our Recruit Training. Some not quite as bad and some too harsh to mention. During these hazing rituals we all thought our instructors were insane, crazy, sadistic. Years later, we would understand that all the insults, the physical abuse and the torment they put us through was not part of a sadistic practice. It was a toughening procedure.

54

We were being trained to work under the harshest and the most objectionable conditions. Like basic military boot camp, our training matched the difficulty of our profession. Our instructors were not sadistic, they were honest. It was their duty to prepare us for a life the likes of which most civilians could never even contemplate.

The training was tough, but it was necessary.

And it worked.

The smell of Scabby's socks brought me back to the present.

"I gotta get some fresh air," I said. As I turned to leave, I heard Rod speak softly to his new friend. "Frank, you're gonna work out just fine. Just fine."

I smiled to myself. Yes, Frank would work out just fine. Then I walked into the Constable's room. I had a telephone call to make.

CHAPTER 7

MOPERY – A CRIME MOST FOUL

THEY HURT OR HEAL,
CREATE GROWTH OR PAIN –
THEY ARE YOUR WORDS.

The Constable's room was empty. I sat at the desk, alone. Our recent encounter with Scabby had all but left my mind. Higgy and Scooter were all that mattered, yet they were things I had no control over.

Higgy had already been hurt — perhaps he would never recover. Scooter would certainly never recover. It was conceivable that, with good counselling and a loving mother, her scars would become bearable. Tragically, her encounter with the inhuman creep that had assaulted her would never truly heal. Even if we caught him, he would be a free man in one-third of whatever prison sentence the judge imposed.

A 10-year term was the best we could hope for. But a 10-year sentence for a crime so brutal was meaningless.

He would be free to offend again a short $3^1/_2$ years after sentencing because most cons become eligible for parole after serving only one-third of their time in a Federal Penitentiary. Eligible for parole usually meant immediate freedom after only a short hearing.

Cons knew how to play the game. If sentenced to "two-years-less-a-day" in a Provincial jail there would be no parole since parole usually was granted only to criminals serving time in a Federal Institution. It was not uncommon for an inmate sentenced to a Provincial jail to assault a guard. His additional one-year sentence would take him to a Federal pen where he would be released after serving only one-third of his sentence. Instead of two years, he would thus serve only one year — a reward for assaulting a guard.

It was a simple ploy that our legislators had never understood.

It was good that our new recruit did not fully understand the judicial system. The Academy had filled his head with hopes that he might some day change the world. Unfortunately, the opposite was true. Some day, the world would change him. He was still young and fresh, full of hope. Scabby had been only a hiccup com-

56

pared to the gut-busting, heart-breaking years ahead.

Pushing aside these thoughts, I reached for the telephone and called Dudzinski, hoping he had turned on his cellular telephone.

"Hey, Stu, it's Bob. How's it going?"

"I'll have the bastard gift-wrapped for you by sunset."

"What?"

"You heard me. I'll have him in custody for you, maybe by supper time. Just gotta find him."

"Who?" He ignored my question. "You found the scene of the crime yet?"

I told him that Bev and I had visited the dump and briefly described the small rubber cup that she had found.

"You just keep what you got. For God's sake tell Bev to hang onto it. I'll call you later," he said, then hung up.

Once on a blood-trail, Dudz rarely spoke to anyone. He was like a bullet fired from a rifle. Single-minded, he would follow only one path, one direction, one trail until it led him to his target. He now had no time for idle chatter. His prey was in sight and his whole being was locked onto his target.

It was nearly noon. I felt sick. My stomach was empty, but I could not eat. It did not matter where I looked, Scooter's face looked back and when the room went quiet I could still hear her voice. Her sobs.

Reaching into my breast pocket for comfort, I ignored a ritual. Poking my fingers through the cotton handkerchief, I found the edge of a single card and withdrew it:

Behind us - only memories,
Ahead of us - only solutions.

Tucking the card back into my pocket, I looked ahead. On the wall someone had hung a poem titled merely, *A Poem For All Police Officers*, written by an unknown author:

"I have been where you all fear to be
and seen what you all fear to see.
I have done the things you fear to do
and all these things I've done for you.

"I am the man you lean upon,
the man you cast your scorn upon,
the man you bring your troubles to
yes, all these things I've been for you.

"The man you ask to stand apart,
the man you feel should have no heart.
The man you call 'the man in blue'
but I'm a man ... a man like you.

"And through the years I've come to see
that I am not what you ask of me.
So take this badge, take this gun.
Will you take it? Will anyone?

"And when you watch a person die
and hear a battered young girl cry
then do you think that I can be
All these things you ask of me?"

I read the poem twice and thought of my career and my life. Inspector King, the officer who had sworn me in, was correct. There would be laughter and tears. Corporal Don Withers was also correct. Life as a Police Officer would be a full life — too full at times. Few people can ever understand the pain, the confusion and the loneliness a cop feels.

I shook off the self-pity and remembered that there was yet a job to do. If I was to keep my promise to Scooter I would have to resume the hunt. My pain was nothing compared to the pain felt by Scooter and her mother.

My reverie was shattered by the bang of the cell door closing.

"Hey, Worm. Like my poem?" Rod led the parade from the cells and had seen me staring at the wall.

"You wrote that?" I asked.

"Naw, but I did operate the photocopier." Everyone laughed. Rod had brought me back to the present and in the company of him, Bev and our new-found friend, Frank, it was a happy present.

Five minutes later we were all back in our cars, looking for an older-model black car with a V-shaped crack in its window and hoping that Higgy would soon open his eyes.

The sun beat down hot upon my police car and I reached over to roll down the window. Briefly, I thought that life was the only game where you could commit no mistakes, yet lose. Higgy had done everything correctly. He had unloaded his revolver prior to arresting a "Mental." He had turned his portable radio on. He had tried reason and verbal persuasion.

He also had been beaten unconscious and now might die for all he did right.

My patrol route took me by two elementary schools and a sports field. I thought our suspect might yet be caught, stalking another child. As my trek took me once again by the police station, my tires chirped as I turned the corner. Denis hated that but I didn't care. I didn't care about anything. It was almost noon and my best friend lay unconscious in a hospital — in a bed I should have been occupying.

58

Suddenly, Bev's voice came over the radio. "Surrey, Bravo 11, request priority. I'm calling in a pursuit!"

"DWEENN" — the alert tone sounded over all police car radios. "Surrey, all cars, Bravo 11 is in pursuit. Keep this channel clear. Bravo 11 you have priority." The "alert tone" that preceded Sharon's voice had clearly announced to all Police Officers on duty to listen carefully for a priority broadcast. In less than five seconds, Sharon had alerted all cars and advised Bev that she now controlled the airwaves.

"Bravo 11 in pursuit of a 1977 Black Cadillac. One occupant. Heading south on Grosvenor Road. Speed in excess of 90 kliks. Cover car, please?" My heart jumped, screamed and pounded inside my chest. Bev had found the suspect vehicle in this morning's rape. Grosvenor Road led directly away from the city dump!

I slammed the accelerator down and felt the blood pounding in my head. I planned to help with this chase. If an arrest was going to be made, I wanted to be a part of it.

"Heading east on 108th now. He's losing me," Bev called.

East on 108th. That meant he would have to turn south on 152 Street or hit the freeway. I chose the freeway option and roared up 176 Street to intercept.

"It's the freeway!" Bev called. "He's going for the freeway. He's eastbound on the freeway! Any cars to intercept?"

"Bravo 23 at 176th and the freeway," I said, as calmly as I could.

"Spike-belt the bastard!" Bev called.

Spike belts were hollow spikes mounted in a wide rubber belt. Spread across the asphalt, they punctured the tires of any vehicle which crossed them. All four tires would then lose air and the vehicle would come to a safe, controlled halt.

"Spike-belt the freeway?" I called back to Bev, suggesting that we'd have 50 cars with flat tires before the Cadillac arrived.

"I don't care. Stop the bastard."

Looking west, I tried to spot the Cadillac but it was still three miles away. The grass median about a quarter mile to the west, however, came alive with a plume of dirt and grass. Then Rod called: "Bravo 16 ... designated ram-car in position, one-half mile west of 176th."

"Take'em, Rod," Bev acknowledged. "I've still got an eyeball on him but he's pulling away."

"10-4 Bevvy. Tighten up your belt, Frank, there's gonna be a bang." Rod had failed to release the microphone button as he spoke to his new recruit. Even the most experienced veterans were not immune to an adrenaline surge in the heat of a high-speed chase.

59

"Shut it down!" Sergeant Denis' voice called over the air. He had heard the chase over his monitor and was about to inflict bad policy on good cops. Senior management always chose to deny Police Officers a successful high-speed chase. We all knew the dangers, the traps and the civil litigation that would follow any car accident resulting from such a chase. We all knew, but we were sworn to uphold the law. Giving up was not an option we considered as easily as our supervisors. "Shut it down!" Denis repeated.

"10-4 Sarge, I'll take him down." Rod rhymed Denis' orders but somehow lost their meaning. It seemed as though the whole Watch were becoming poets and Denis had been reduced to an impotent leader of Police Officers who could not, or would not, hear him.

Looking westward, what I saw belonged in a cowboy movie. Our recruit, Frank, was driving Bravo 16 and had flanked the black Cadillac. Matching his speed, Rod leaned out the passenger's window and pointed his shotgun at the driver's face. The big old car slowed and pulled over to the side of the freeway.

"Would somebody give me a B.C.L.?" Sharon called.

"Sierra - Lima - Hotel - 1-9-6." Frank read out the British Columbia license plate of the now-still car. Frank had become a veteran cop in the space of one morning. Both his training and ability to listen to Rod were put to the test. It was apparent even as he spoke.

"High-risk take down gentlemen," Rod said, over the radio. Then he added, "Take your positions."

Rather than approach and restrict their firing angle, I stayed in my car approximately 200 yards ahead, ready to ram the offending vehicle if it attempted an escape. It was my task to ensure the high-speed chase did not resume. Rod was only half-joking when he had called in his car as the "designated ram car."

But I wasn't in a joking mood. I was prepared and committed to ram this vehicle broadside if it had attempted to escape.

"Bravo 11's on your tail, guys, take him down." Bev had slid to a stop behind Bravo 16 and sat still, her door open. She had not approached on foot because she did not want to distract Rod or Frank, yet with her door open she could be there in seconds. In addition, by remaining behind the wheel of her car she could resume the chase instantly if he sped off.

Rod's voice came over the loudspeaker of Bravo 16. "Driver of the black Cadillac. Listen carefully. You will do exactly as I say. Throw your car keys out your window and leave both your hands outside the car, palms up, where I can see them."

A set of keys arced out the window and both hands remained

60

plainly visible. Rod had his own style and he departed from standard operating procedures. Carrying the shotgun, he left the passenger's seat, quickly ran around the rear of his police car and took cover behind the driver's door.

"Pass me the loud-hailer microphone, Frank," Rod ordered. Taking the microphone in hand, he rested the shotgun on the top of his driver's door. "Now remain motionless. Keep your hands palms-up and leave them outside the window where I can see them. Don't move a muscle or I'll blow your goddamned head off." Slowly he approached the car. Frank followed, gun drawn, a few steps behind.

"Take him out," Rod ordered.

Carefully, Frank holstered his gun and opened the driver's door of the Cadillac. In one fluid move he grabbed the driver by the side of his collar and jerked him from the seat and threw him face-down in the gravel. Quickly, he planted his knee firmly between the driver's shoulder blades and applied the handcuffs. Frank looked at Rod for approval. Rod ignored him and instead knelt down beside his prey.

Through a pair of binoculars I had seen the situation was now under control. Driving the wrong way on the gravel shoulder, I pulled up in front of the black Cadillac and exited my vehicle. With a smile on my face, I watched Rod take charge.

"If you haven't noticed it, asshole, you're under arrest!"

Bev had since approached on foot. She was trembling. "You got the bastard! You got him!"

"Look again, Bev," Rod said.

The driver was only a teenager. The pimples on his face matched the gravel that still stuck to his oily skin as he looked up in fear. "It's my Dad's car. I didn't steal it. It's my Dad's car."

Our hopes were dashed. Bev's face grew angry, as she realized that Scooter's assailant was still at large.

Frank had already handcuffed and placed the young boy into the back of their car. Rod assessed the situation. "His father won't appear as a court witness for auto theft. Since this kid doesn't have a driver's license, the courts will call him a young offender and he will get a suspended sentence. Ain't worth the gas to drive him back to the cells."

Bev nodded. Her fists were clenched and her lips were drawn. Adrenaline surged through her body. Her heart raced and her blood pressure rose out of control. All of us felt that way after a high-speed chase. Too many Police Officers had been badly injured or killed during chases that had gone wrong. Yet we felt compelled to risk our lives and finish what the perpetrator had started. Bev had just risked her life chasing Scooter's assailant. The result was that she was facing a pimple-faced youth who had gone for a ride in his father's car.

Many people can never understand the emotions, the fears and the anger we experience both during and after a high-speed chase. They criticize us for chasing suspect vehicles. Bev was not chasing a young lad who took his father's car without consent. She was chasing a rapist who had violated a young girl's life. She was chasing a less-than-human pervert who had brutalized poor Scooter. She was chasing pure evil.

She had caught, however, a young pimple-faced lad. Bev was nearly out of control. All she could do was clench her teeth and her fists. "That's it?" she screamed. "That's it!"

Bev had risked her life in a needless chase and rage had taken over. It was a rage that couldn't be understood unless experienced. Cops hate high-speed chases almost as much as they hate the criticism that inevitably follows.

Walking over to Rod's car, she grabbed the boy by his shoulders and held him tight. She leaned half-inside the rear compartment and screamed, "You little piss-ant. I ought to strip the skin off you and roll you in salt. You should be whipped until your eyes bleed. Why, I ought to take you out of this car and throw you in front of the first truck that rolls by."

Her fists gripped his shirt and her arms held him rigid until her muscles began to metabolize the adrenaline. "We ought to lock you up so tight they'll have to pipe in the sunshine and feed you with a slingshot."

The boy began to sob, then the tears flowed. "Why I ought to ram five pounds of hamburger meat down your throat and shove a pit bull up your arse!"

Bev shoved him back and slammed the door. The scene seemed brutal by most people's standards. Bev had not shaken or assaulted him in any manner. She had hardly even sworn at him. Her only crime was that she had threatened him with promises he knew she would never keep. We do not apologize for this behavior, nor do we condone it. But we do understand that it exists. She had not been brutal to him. She had not even scared him as much as he had scared her. We do, however, hope that one day, people will understand our actions, our fears, and forgive us.

The young boy had, in his brief reckless tour through the streets of Surrey, put many lives at risk. He was lucky this time and we knew that should he continue this type of behavior, eventually he would kill innocent people or die himself.

This rage that follows a high-speed chase was common. Any

62

experienced Police Officer understood. This young lad's father, however, did not. When the boy later told him about the five pounds of hamburger, Bev received a formal caution on her record. For the remainder of her career her personal file stated: "This police officer remains indifferent to instructions and possesses an over-zealous attitude." Although these remarks did not sound bad, they were devastating.

In the rhetoric of upper management, "indifferent to instructions" meant "She thinks she knows more than her seniors." "Over-zealous attitude" meant "opinionated and brazen." Ironically, these words summarized Bev's character — intelligent and opinionated. Perfect qualities for a Police Officer who must make decisions in an instant which would take upper management, lawyers and judges months or years to decide if they were appropriate.

Unfortunately, many members of the public rarely understand that our decisions, most made in life-and-death situations, are not always perfect. Our decisions are based on survival. We don't have the luxury of debating whether they are judicially correct or not.

I walked over to Bev and tried to calm her. She was more upset than I had ever seen.

"Hell, Bob, it ain't the chase. I thought I had him. I thought I had the bastard. Now this! I'll probably get dumped on for what I did."

"Ya, you will. But that's okay."

Bev looked at Rod. "You taking him back?"

"Sure, Bev. We'll give him a room across from Scabby."

"I wish," Bev said. "She knew that as a 'young offender' this prisoner would be given his own private cell.

Rod turned to Bev. "Don't worry, Sweetie. I'm gonna scare the hormones outa this kid. He's about to grow up real quick. He is about to receive a history lesson. See you in cells."

We climbed back into our cars and headed off the freeway.

"Surrey, Bravo 16," Rod called.

"Go ahead 16."

"We're R.T.O. with a prisoner." Rod explained he was Returning To the Office with his young offender. "Call Walt in cells, please. Tell him to hang the rules in plain sight. He'll know what you mean."

"10-4. Already seen it," Sharon acknowledged.

Ten minutes later, Bev and I watched in the cellblock. Frank was preparing the booking-in sheet while Rod supervised.

"Y'know, young fella. You're in a heap o' hurt."

"Why?" the boy asked as his cuffs were taken off and he cleaned the gravel from his face.

63

"The charge."

"What charge? Speeding? It was my old man's car. Got no theft rap on me."

"The charge," Rod repeated.

"The charge?" The boy's face portrayed a seriousness that had not been present a moment earlier.

"The Charge!" Rod emphasized. His face grew serious as he spoke. "You are under arrest for mopery. It is my duty to warn you that you are not obliged to say anything and anything you say will be given as evidence. You have the right to retain and instruct counsel without delay. A Legal Aid Duty lawyer is available to provide legal advice to you if you so desire. If you wish to contact a Legal Aid Duty lawyer, I can provide you with a telephone number.

"Mopery?" the boy asked, ignoring everything else. "What's mopery?"

"A very grave offense under the Young Offender's Act. Section 357, subsection 1(a), paragraph 3, subparagraph 3(b)." Rod quoted from a memory he was in the process of constructing. "Mopery. Anyone between the age of 16 and 19 who commits mopery, is, notwithstanding the provisions of the Federal Statutes and related Sub-statutes heretofore and hereinafter enacted upon and as heretofore stated, restated and stated again in the event you were not listening, is guilty of an indictable offense. He is subject to immediate imprisonment for a period of not less than one year. Whether or not the aforementioned was concurrent with the present condition or whatever. And," Rod added in a most serious voice, "may God have mercy upon your soul."

"Mopery." Rod confirmed the charge then looked at the wall over the counter. "You're gonna be with us for a while young feller, better get used to it."

Posted on the wall was a set of 10 simple rules, titled "RULES FOR COMMON JAIL PRISONERS". Below the title, 10 simple rules for behavior were listed:

"1. THE FIRST DUTY OF A PRISONER IS STRICT OBEDIENCE.

"2. STRICT SILENCE SHALL BE OBSERVED; PRISONERS SHALL NOT SPEAK TO ONE ANOTHER.

"3. PRISONERS SHALL ALWAYS APPROACH ALL JAIL OFFICIALS IN A RESPECTFUL MANNER, SPEAK IN A RESPECTFUL TONE OF VOICE AND IN AS FEW WORDS AS POSSIBLE MAKE KNOWN THEIR REQUEST.

"4. WHEN CALLED TO ATTENTION, PRISONERS SHALL ASSUME THAT POSITION, LOOKING STRAIGHT TO THE FRONT.

64

"5. PRISONERS SHALL, AT ALL TIMES, LOOK STRAIGHT TO THEIR FRONT IN GOING TO AND RETURNING FROM WORK.

"6. EVERY PRISONER SHALL SWEEP OUT HIS CELL THOROUGHLY UPON GETTING UP, EMPTY HIS SLOP PAIL AND MAKE UP HIS BED IN THE REGULATION MANNER AND NO PRISONER SHALL ON ANY PRETEXT ENTER THE CELL OF ANOTHER.

"7. EVERY PRISONER SHALL KEEP HIS CELL NEAT AND CLEAN.

"8. EVERY PRISONER SHALL KEEP HIS CLOTHES IN REPAIR AND NEAT AND TIDY.

"9. PRISONERS WILL NOT BE ALLOWED TO HOLD COMMUNICATION WITH ANY PERSON OR PERSONS EXCEPT AS FOLLOWS:

"Any person desiring to see any prisoner on a weekday will be permitted to do so after obtaining a special permit from the Jailer. On Sunday afternoons, persons may be admitted without permit from 2 to 4 p.m., provided they are known to the Jailer to be quiet and respectable persons.

"All interviews will be held in the presence of the Jailer or Assistant Jailer and shall not exceed ten minutes on weekdays and fifteen minutes on Sundays, except in special cases wherein an extension may be made by the Jailer's authority.

"10. NO LOCAL NEWSPAPERS OF ANY KIND WILL BE ALLOWED IN THE PRISON AND ALL OTHER READING MATTER SHALL PASS THE PROVOST'S INSPECTION BEFORE IT IS GIVEN TO THE PRISONERS."

We watched as the young lad's eyes grew as big as the hub caps on Bravo 16. Fortunately, he had not read the small inscription at the bottom of the poster. It read: "ROYAL NORTH-WEST MOUNTED POLICE — 1915."

The young boy stood completely motionless as he read the rules one by one. A tear ran down his face and, mixed with the road dirt, created a tiny mud puddle.

"Mopery," he said and began to cry. "I'll never see my parents again." He sobbed, then his knees buckled and he fell to the floor.

Rod reached down and picked him up. "Young fella, you have committed a crime most grave. Your sentence may not be as long as you anticipate but it begins now. I'm about to take you to your cell where you will have several hours to contemplate your fate. Are you listening?" A young head nodded.

"I'll be back to see you before sunset. In the next few hours I want you to consider the crime you have committed. See those offi-

65

cers?" Rod pointed in the direction of Bev, Frank and me. "See them? They should be out on the street."

His finger swept toward the exit of the cell block. "Out on the street. We have some very serious work to do today and you just plumb got in the way. We don't take kindly to the likes of you. Come with me now, you're about to begin your sentence."

The young mud-faced youth looked at us directly. "I'm sorry. I'll never mope again. Does this mean I won't get my comics to read in prison?" None of us laughed or even smiled. In an instant we realized that from his point of view he faced life imprisonment. Even one year for a young boy was life imprisonment. Life imprisonment without comics.

The three of us watched solemnly as Rod led the young man to his cell. We listened as he threw the iron bars closed and turned the key. Together we eavesdropped as Rod admonished his prisoner. "You just sit here and think about what you've done. I'll be back before sundown to deal with you. You're not a bad kid, y'know, but you've done something very bad that must be dealt with. I'd be willing to waive all charges, maybe, if you can show me you're worth it." Then he added, "I'll see you later."

"Yes, sir," a young voice answered.

Rod reappeared from the cells. "Can you believe it? He's still standing at attention. I'll let him stew for a couple hours then call his folks. Sure don't like to hurt him like I did, but maybe the shock will do him good."

We all stood silent. This was a ploy that was used often on young prisoners. Sometimes it worked — sometimes it did not. It was a fairly safe gamble, though, and designed to help a young boy grow up quickly. When it worked, it changed a person's outlook permanently. When it didn't work, it meant he was already experienced in the ways of a criminal and knew the entire scenario was a bluff.

Either way, the gamble was small and the rewards potentially great.

"C'mon guys," Bev spoke. "We've got some work to do."

There were six hours left in a shift that so far had been far from routine.

66

CHAPTER 8

COCKATOOS AND LORIKEETS — BIRDNAPPED

THE KINDEST DEED YOU CAN DO
IS TO HELP ANOTHER PERSON –
AND NOT GET DISCOVERED.

I pulled out of the parking lot with thoughts of lunch. I wasn't hungry, but I felt that a greasy hamburger pounded down with a cup of extra strong, extra sweet coffee would take my mind away from thoughts of Higgy and Scooter. Although it was only noon, we had already booked in two prisoners. That was rare for day shift. Taking prisoners was our night-time activity. Day shift in the cell block was normally quiet, except for the arrival of a few prisoners who would appear for trial. Today was different. Today we had already caught the dirtiest and the saddest.

Prisoners, however, rarely bothered me. They had chosen the path that led to our cells. On only very rare occasions could I find compassion for prisoners, though a few had tugged at my heart. Over the many years I had seen a large assortment — common drunks, shoplifters, drug addicts, armed robbers and murderers. Most of them had become faceless names and nameless faces. All crowded together in a mind that tried to forget.

Forgetting them was easy. All I had to do was take my memories and shove them away in a special place I had reserved in my mind. But like most Police Officers, I couldn't really completely dismiss them. The headaches that I felt all too often told me that this "special place" was becoming too crowded. Doctors and psychologists have a name for this phenomenon. They call it "stress." Naming it, however, wasn't a cure, and as the years passed it was becoming a more noticeable part of me.

Reaching down to my CAD head, I punched the police radio with one finger. "R.T.T." (Request to talk.)

"Bravo 23." Sharon acknowledged my call.

"Am I clear?"

"10-4," she acknowledged, then added, "stand-by one, I've got one call left on the stack. It's a low priority, Bob, can you take it?"

67

"Lay it on me."

"It's a break-in. Reported to our office zero eight hundred hours. I would have given it to you earlier but you were busy."

"10-4, thanks Sharon. Go ahead with details."

"Break-in. Occurred overnight at Birds "R" Us. Pet Store at 101 Street and Old Yale Road. Owner's name is Kenneth Wilson. States the break-in occurred overnight and a quantity of stock was taken. Owner was quite upset. Has called back three times. Like I said, Bob, he's pretty upset. Can I call him and advise your E.T.A.?"

"10-4 Sharon. I'll just make a quick detour by Surrey Memorial Hospital then straight to this call. He's only a couple of blocks from the hospital."

"Received. Time dispatched is zero thirteen hundred hours. And let us know how Higgy's doing, will you? Please? We're all sitting on pins and needles in the radio room."

Five minutes later I parked my car at the hospital and walked into Higgy's room.

It was empty. Over the bed was a hand-scrawled sign which read: "MRI." They had taken Bruce's unconscious body to Magnet Resonance Imaging. It was a new machine that could map the brain and portray it as slices on a computer screen. I looked at the empty bed and wondered if the computer images could ever reveal the thoughts, the hopes, the dreams, the wishes of the man who had taken my place.

Unfortunately, modern technology was limited to mapping blood vessels and tumors. Higgy was just another computer image.

"He's going to be gone a while." Nurse Jane had popped her head around the corner. "There's no change."

"C'mon, Jane. That's a stock answer. Please? He's my buddy and...."

"Yes, I understand. You cops are like nurses. It's a family, I know. Look, Bob, he's undergoing every test they can administer. They've poked him, prodded him, X-rayed him, he's got more tubes in him than an underground lawn sprinkler. He's had the best of care. In fact, they usually reserve the MRI test until after 48 hours. It is expensive and there is always a line up. If it wasn't for some good Samaritan he'd be lying there for you to visit. Seems like Higgy has friends in high places but they sure are cantankerous. Our nurses' station has been getting a call nearly every hour, even through the night. Somewhat annoying except...."

"Except what?"

"Well, whoever his guardian angel is, he has money. Says he'll pay for whatever the RCMP doesn't. He's already talked to

68

our Hospital Administrator and I've been advised that Higgy is to receive V.I.P. status. I think there'll be some private billing on this."

"Who the hell would do that? Higgy isn't rich. He doesn't even know anybody who is. Hell, Higgy's just a cop."

"I don't know. Someone named Denee or something similar. Says he knows you and told us to sneak you into the room if you showed up."

Denee! Denee! Bruce's benefactor was, in reality, Sergeant Denis. He was of French heritage, although his family name had been Anglicized. Denis! My eyes filled, my world spun, the roar in my ears reminded me of all the unkind things I had ever said to him. Denis was proud of his French heritage — even threatened to learn French some day.

"Denis!" I said out loud. "What the hell...."

"You mean what the heaven. This Denee person offers a buffer of $10,000 for Bruce's tests and adds that he won't be in to visit.

"Why not?"

"He says he doesn't belong. Bruce should wake up looking into the eyes of a friend. Bob, don't tell anyone what I've said. This sort of thing rarely happens and when it does, we have to keep it secret. Other patients would get jealous, you know. It's worth my job if anyone found out I told you."

"Don't worry, Jane, you're safe."

She nodded and smiled.

"Thanks, Jane," I said as I slowly started to leave. "You don't know just how much you've helped." Then I added, "All of us."

Somehow Sergeant Denis had become a different person. I suddenly felt guilty about interrupting his briefings and for the ill feelings I held for him. I would always be grateful to a man of whom I had sworn to be an enemy. Worse, there was my promise to Jane and its heavy burden of never being able to say thank you to him.

I could never betray nurse Jane's trust. Yet somehow, somewhere, some day I silently promised myself to repay the debt. I would return the kindness that Sergeant Denis had held so secret.

"I'll call when Higgy gets back." Jane offered.

"Thanks, Jane." I waved, then left the ward.

Ten minutes later I pulled into the parking lot of a small pet store — Birds "R" Us. I noted a sign as I walked up to the door. It had been hand-scrawled and hung at eye level. It read, bleakly: "CLOSED — OUT OF BUSINESS."

Something's fishy here, my instinct immediately told me. A store gets broken into then goes out of business. Sounds like he

69

was planning to close down and decided to collect on the insurance.

It was a common occurrence. A businessman, already financially distressed, would merely order extra stock, asking for extended credit from his suppliers. The stock would be sold out the back door to other stores, then the owner would take a pry bar to the rear door and claim he had been broken into. The money owing on the stock would be forgiven in bankruptcy court, and the insurance money would finance another business or provide a wonderful holiday for the store owner.

"Out of business, my arse," I said to myself. Talking to oneself was a diversion that most Police Officers practiced. It was easier than talking to criminals, complainants and many people who composed most of our daily contacts.

I knocked on the door.

No answer.

A louder knock still brought no answer.

Not wanting to clear this call, only having to return later, I walked to the alley behind the building. The rear door of the pet store was open. For a moment I thought I might find the owner loading sacks of pet food and cages of hamsters into a waiting truck.

But there was no activity at all.

Slowly, I approached the rear door and stood silent. Perhaps the break-in was genuine and the perpetrators had returned?

Then I heard something. A strange sound. Was someone crying? I listened closer.

There was no doubt.

Someone inside the door was sobbing. It was the most pitiful sound I had ever heard. A grown man was crying as though he had just lost his entire family and been banished from the planet. It wasn't a cry of physical pain — it was the cry of a tortured soul. The sound of crying is something with which a Police Officer gains a great deal of familiarity. Women, children, men, teenagers — all have their own sounds. This one was of a grown man perhaps in his mid-twenties.

Entering the store, I softly called, "Police. Hello? Police. Someone called for the police?" Patiently, I waited for a response.

From a small storage room a young man in his early twenties appeared. He had taken the time to dry his eyes, but they were red and swollen. He blew his nose as he walked up and offered his hand as a greeting.

"Hello, Officer," he said between sobs, "my name is Ken, Ken Wilson. I am glad you came. I am sorry to bother you but I don't

70

know who to talk to." He wiped his eyes with his hand and then held it out to greet me.

I shook his hand briefly, wiped his tears on the side of my trousers and listened to his tale.

Sometime during the night, one or more thieves had entered his store and stolen most of the contents. Between sobs, he related that he had been totally cleaned out. Ten bags of millet, 10 bags of canary seed, five bags of sunflower seeds, medicines and pet potions, five diatomaceous earth aquarium filters, 23 bird cages — the list went on for nearly five minutes.

After listening to Ken's near endless list of missing supplies, I asked why he was so upset. Surely his insurance would cover at least part of his loss?

He began to cry again. Between sobs he said, "It's Cuddles. Cuddles. They took Cuddles. And they took Tweedledee and Tweedledumb." His tears flowed freely.

Repressing a smile, I asked who they were.

"My kids," he sobbed.

I was shocked. My spine stiffened and I could feel anger and fear rising inside. He had left his children in the store overnight and I was four hours late responding to a kidnapping?

"My kids," he continued. "I've had them since they were eggs. Hand-brooded and hand-raised them. For five years we've never spent a day apart. Now they're gone! Gone! I know you'll never get them back for me."

Cuddles, he explained, was a Moluccan Cockatoo — a big white Salmon-Crested Cockatoo weighing over five pounds. He had a beak that could remove a finger but had never inflicted even a nip on Ken or any store customer. "He's a big white Teddy Bear," Ken sobbed. "Never been hurt and he's never hurt anyone."

Tweedledee and Tweedledumb, on the other hand, were two small, yet incredibly colorful Lorikeets, or Lories as they were commonly called. They were a mere seven inches long, but their bright red, blue and green coloring made them an attraction wherever they perched. The Lorikeets could survive for only a day or two in their new home. They needed a well-heated shelter and lived on a mixture of sweetened baby food and sweet fruits such as small white grapes. Oranges or lemons would most certainly make them sick and they would not even attempt to eat bird seed.

Ken had purchased them when they were eggs and through careful monitoring successfully helped them through their "birthing" process, breaking away the egg bit-by-bit when nature indicated it was "hatch-day."

Over the next three months he fed them every 45 minutes, 24

71

hours a day, slowly weaning them of his hand-rearing and painstakingly showing them how to feed themselves.

Ken proudly showed me photos of the young bald birds, sleeping contentedly in their nests, each with a tiny Teddy Bear of its own. Then, as their feathers grew, a succession of photos showed how they matured and followed him wherever he went. They bathed with him, drove in the car with him and even, on occasion, slept beside him on his pillow.

I had never thought birds could be so happy, so affectionate and so childlike. The Lorikeets took turns riding in his shirt pocket, with Cuddles perched on his shoulder wherever he went.

"My kids," he said as he dried his eyes. "They come when I call them, do a few tricks and always greet me in the morning. I can replace all this stock. I've got enough money salted away for that, but I can't go on. My family's gone and...." He began to cry.

I had always thought that birds were things that sat in trees and pooped on cars. I had never known them to be happy little souls. Nor had I ever suspected that they would result in one of the most gut-wrenching and career-damning calls I would ever accept.

I felt sorry for Ken. His grief was real, although many people could never understand his anguish over the loss of three birds. Against my better judgement, I made a promise I knew I might not be able to keep. My word was given that we would get his family back. Every informant on my list would be squeezed "until their eyes bled" if necessary. He reminded me we had only 48 hours but little did we know that less than six hours remained before the birds would be killed and disposed of.

I knew action had to be taken immediately. From my notebook I picked a telephone number and dialled it carefully. "Mikey, it's Bob. You busy?"

"No," he answered.

"Look, I'll make this simple for you. Want to get off the drug rap you got yourself into last week?" It is not commonly known, but on occasion Police Officers are willing to throw a small fish back into the lake in order to leave room in their boat for a bigger one.

Mikey was a no-good person — a slimy, gutter-crawling sewer rat. He had spent most of his life in jail and between sentences survived by finking on his peers and pimping for young teenaged girls. Mikey had no honor, brains or morality. Using Mikey made me feel dirty but there would be plenty of time for taking a bath once the job was done.

"Listen, Mikey, last night someone took some birds from...." Mikey finished my sentence, describing the birds and the store.

72

"I want them back, Mikey. I want them back real bad. You got one charge about to send you away. I'll withdraw that charge in exchange for three birds."

"I don't know," he faltered. " Pretty heavy dude that took them. He's an Angel." Damn, my hopes faded as my would-be informant told me the culprit was a member of Hell's Angels. This was going to be a tough one.

"Look, Mikey, I'll meet you half way on this. Don't bother telling me who, just tell me where."

"Where what?"

"Where the birds are, you brainless idiot. Mikey, I just want the birds. You don't have to get dirty on this one. You already know where they are, don't you?"

"Yup. Seen them, too. Sure are pretty but that big one looks mean."

"Look, Mikey, just tell me where they are and I'll let you off the hook."

Mickey quickly made a decision. "1520 Lord Byron Road."

"That's the Flats. The birds are there now?"

"They are."

"And the occupant of the house?"

"Sinbad. I'm gonna set him up for a sale tonight. Says if he can't sell them today he's gonna ring their puny necks and bury them. Says they're too noisy and doesn't want to draw any heat to his house." Mikey obviously was already involved in the crime.

"Move up your meeting time to this afternoon," I said.

"I don't know, it'll be hard."

"Look, Mikey, you got two girls working for you, right?"

"Yaaaa," he replied cautiously. He wasn't aware that he had been the subject of a stakeout near the roller rink and had been seen pimping for two teenage runaways.

"Want one month's amnesty in addition to your drug charge being dropped."

"Yaaaa."

"Then make the meeting for 2:00 p.m. Make sure Sinbad goes to the meeting and leaves the birds at home." I already had a plan so rotten it could never be placed on any police report.

"I'll phone you back in five," he said, and hung up.

For the next few minutes I explained to Ken that there was a good possibility he would be reunited with his "family" in a very short time.

"God. You can have anything in the store." He began to cry again. Family reunions, I thought, are always emotional affairs.

"Naw, I just want to see your family back together again." I

73

had never before seen this kind of love and it felt good. Ken had worked 24 hours a day, seven days a week and cared for his charges. None of the three missing children would ever be sold. They were his family.

"How you going to do it?" he asked.

"Don't ask." I was reluctant to confess to the crime I was about to commit. It could see the end of my career. Perhaps even a jail term.

The telephone rang. "Meeting is set for 2:00 p.m. at the Flamingo. He should be out for an hour."

"Thanks, Mikey. If your word is good, you got a free Get-out-of-jail card coming to you."

"It's good. Don't screw with me."

"Thanks, Mikey." I bid Ken good-bye and asked him to stay in the store until 6 o'clock.

I sat in my police car and began to polish off the rough edges of my plan. If it were to succeed it would have to be done fast and secretly. In addition, I would need assistance of a fellow Police Officer who was as sly as me. I needed help from someone I could trust implicitly. Picking up my mike, I called, "Surrey, Bravo 23, mark me 10-6 on this call for an hour or so would you, please?"

"10-4, Bob. I'll have to clear it with the Sarge though, but that'll take a while. He's spent most of the morning on the telephone."

I smiled. Only I and nurse Jane and every neurologist in Vancouver knew what he was up to.

"10-4. Thanks, Sharon." I suspected Sergeant Denis was calling in every favor he could just to ensure Bruce Higgins received the best medical attention possible. Briefly, I thought that he would have been the perfect partner in the plan I had formulated. But he was busy.

I knew who I would ask for help. Constable Gord Schneider. I had known Gord for many years. He was never the greatest investigator, but he was better than most. His honor, however, was his finest attribute. He would go anywhere, do anything and suffer everything if he thought he could help another person. Gord was a perfect choice for the crime we were about to commit.

"Bravo 23, Bravo 10."

"Bravo 10."

"Gord, how'd you like to boogey back to the office, pick up an unmarked car, two pairs of coveralls and meet me behind the Turf."

Being careful not to tie up the airwaves or give out too many details over the police radio, I explained that I needed his help on

74

a sensitive investigation. I knew Gord would trust my judgement. It was no surprise that he agreed to help — no questions asked.

He would procure an unmarked police car and meet me behind the Turf Hotel within 30 minutes.

Taking the shortest route possible, I drove to the Turf and parked in the northwest corner of the lot. As I waited, I thought of Scooter, Higgy and Sergeant Denis who had made the transition from enemy to friend.

Our relationship had changed and I was confused. Sergeant Denis had not changed. Only my perception of him had altered. He was the same man that he was during briefing, but now I had learned his true identity. Denis was human, just like the rest of us. We had only to recognize that simple fact and all the dislike, all the hatred, disappeared.

I removed the Deck of cards from my breast pocket.

Shuffle. Cut. Turn over top card:

You can never do a kindness too soon —
because you never know when it will be too late.

Thinking of the death sentence Cuddles and his other feathered companions were awaiting made my stomach tighten. Nothing to do but wait for Gord.

To me the Deck was magic. Ask it a question and it gave an answer. No one ever needed to be alone, confused or without answers as long as he or she had a Deck like mine. For a moment, I closed my eyes and thanked Corporal Don Withers. He rode in my briefcase and breast pocket every day of my service. He knew everything — everything except how to stop the bullet that punched a hole in his chest a few months after he left the Academy. But he still lived in the 52 hand-written cards I carried. Each card, like Don, contained the truth in the simplest of words.

Summoning the courage to take a double-dose of the truth, I held the cards and asked if my plan to recover Ken's family was an honorable one. As I had done countless times, I shuffled the Deck, cut it and turned over the top card:

Fight fire with fire —
treachery with treachery and —
cowardice with courage.

In those words I found the courage to detail the fine points of my plan.

Mikey had told me where the birds were kept. If I was to obtain a search warrant, details of my informant may be requested. Based on such unproven grounds, no Justice of the Peace would

75

ever grant a warrant to search a house for three birds. Application for a search warrant would, therefore, make a search impossible. Once denied, an unlawful search would be a foolhardy attempt. A fighter never advertises his next move.

No, a search warrant would be impossible. The search had to be conducted covertly. For this reason, Sinbad could never be arrested or charged. To admit to a covert search would mean the end of a career and likely a criminal charge against me.

Yet it was a safe plan — if we did not get caught. Sinbad would most likely not report the break-in and Constable Schneider would never inform on me. Yes. A good plan executed by sympathetic cops.

Interrupting my thoughts, an old black prisoner van pulled into the parking lot and stopped beside me.

"Hey, Bobo. Couldn't get the "suits" to loan me an unmarked car so I stole this beater from Gerry." Gord had arrived in a condemned prisoner van he had borrowed from our Police Transport Manager. It was an unmarked Ford van. Peppered with rust spots and dents, it blended in perfectly with this neighborhood.

"Got the coveralls?" I asked.

"Yup." He didn't ask why.

"Meet me by the boat yard." We left the parking lot and a moment later donned our coveralls.

"I'll leave Bravo 23 here. It ought to be safe for a while."

"Hey, you still haven't told me what this is all about."

Climbing into the passenger's side, I explained my plan. In the next hour, Sinbad would leave his house. Hopefully, there would be nobody home. As quickly as possible we would enter....

"Enter?" Gord interrupted. "Enter? As in bust into the place?"

"Penetrate." I chose a softer word.

I explained my plan and waited for his reply.

"What are we waiting for?" he asked.

Ten minutes later we sat in the 1500 block of Lord Byron Road watching an old tumble-down, wood-frame house. In a few minutes the roar of a Harley-Davidson pounded off the nearby houses and a dust plume signalled the departure of our birdnapper.

Gord pulled the van into the driveway and turned off the engine. "What'll we do if there is someone home?" he asked.

"Hadn't thought of that. We'll probably be okay, I saw one of his girls, Hooters, hooking up by the Roller Rink earlier today. She was the only prostitute working day shift. I think she's the only one living here with Sinbad."

I was wrong.

There was no answer to our knocking so in one move Gord

76

raised his leg. "We'll use the search warrant I've got written on the sole of my shoe."

The door flew open, slammed closed, then flew open again.

Two pit bulls stared at us and lunged. Reaching into my pocket I pulled out an aerosol can of HALT and pressed until a stream of greasy brown liquid wet down both dogs. The spray used by the Postal Service causes little pain but instantly forms a thick scum on the dog's eyes, effectively blinding them for an hour or so.

In confusion, the guard dogs zig-zagged their way to the street and were gone.

"Keep it tight, Bobo, he's likely got some booby traps waiting for us."

"Ya," I answered, as we slowly walked into the house, fanning our flashlights across the floors, walls and ceiling of the dimly lit hallway.

"Sshhh!" Gord suddenly cautioned. "Sshhh! Listen! Bingo!" We both smiled as the slate-screech that only a Lorikeet could make raked our ears.

Ten minutes later Gord drove silently out of the driveway. "What a fitting way to retire a prisoner van," he said. "Full of prisoners."

"Prisoners?"

"Yes. Prisoners. Six Quail, 25 Hamsters, eight Guinea pigs, five rabbits, two snakes, a basket of lizards and four tarantulas."

"And a partridge in a pear tree!" I sang.

"Naw, just a bunch of boxes of aquarium filters and about 15 bags of seeds."

I nodded my head up and down. We had broken the law. While purists would condemn us for our action, I hoped that the public would understand. Justice had been done, even if the law was bent. The memory of Corporal Don Withers drifted into my mind, along with his directions.

"As Police Officers, you are not merely enforcing the law. You are enforcing ideals. Always ensure you are serving only the highest of ideals — and principles." I knew we had broken the law and that punishment, if we were discovered, would be most severe. But I had been taught that the law is not an impersonal set of rules printed on paper. The law is a code, established to protect people — and animals.

As these thoughts cleared from my mind, I heard a voice I would never forget. Coming from the back of the prisoner van, I could hear someone laughing.

"Ha, ha, ha, Give me a kiss, you big white lump! Ha, ha, ha." It was Cuddles, saying thanks as only a Cockatoo could.

77

"How we gonna do this?" Gord asked. "What plans do you have for returning the birds?"

"Well, we don't have to worry about Sinbad. I saw that note you left scrawled in lipstick on his mirror." Gord had left a simple sign which read: "Rot in Hell Asshole. Hands off the Birds or Die!"

That would scare the biker. To know his house was vulnerable, with a death threat held over him from someone he did not know, would certainly lure him away from the birds to other, safer crimes. Worse, he would receive no support from his fellow bikers. To fail at a crime as simple as birdnapping was contemptible. In addition to that, even bikers had a code of ethics. We had outfoxed Sinbad at his own game. There would be no retribution from Sinbad and we would seek no penalty.

"The .38 caliber shell you left stuck on the mirror should make that point clear," Gord said.

"We won this round," I agreed. Somehow I think Sinbad is man enough to take defeat gracefully.

We drove to the boat yard where I picked up Bravo 23 and followed Gord.

Fifteen minutes later we arrived at the pet store. I walked up to Gord's car as he rolled his window down. "Gord, let me do this please?" I asked.

"Look, Bob, I'll go you one better Go inside. Talk to Ken. Give me 10 minutes before you break the news. I'll have all the feed, the filters and the cages stacked up against the side of the store and I'll place all the animals in a circle with the 'three kids' in the center. It'll be like Christmas."

A lump formed in my throat as I anticipated one of the happiest times of my life. "You're a good man, Gord. You know we'll never get credit for this bust? We can't ever tell anyone about it. You understand that, don't you."

"That's what makes it so much fun," Gord smiled. Then he added, "The kindest deed you can do is to help another person and not get discovered. Now you go on in there and have some fun."

I turned my back on the sound of cages rattling, boxes scraping on the metal floor of the van and a gruff voice saying, "Ha, ha, ha, Give me a kiss, you big white lump."

Without knocking, I opened the rear door to the pet shop and closed it behind me. I did not want Ken to hear anyone asking for a kiss. Not for 10 minutes, at least.

"You're back!" Ken's face lit up, then his jaw dropped and his lips parted. I was alone.

"Well, Ken, it's not as bad as it seems. Let me explain something to you."

78

"No, thanks. Hey, I appreciate you trying. I just gotta be alone now."

For the next 10 minutes I uncomfortably intruded on his mourning. He had lost the best friends he ever had. His business was finished and his family gone. Then a loud squeal of tires announced Gord's departure. Everything was now stacked near the back door.

"Look, Bob," Ken began to cry again. "I just want to be alone now. Please?"

"Okay, Ken," I agreed. "But before I go, could you just show me the pry marks on the back door again?"

Weighted down with sorrow, he slowly walked to the back door.

"Open the door for me, would ya'?" I asked.

"Huh?"

"Just open the door." My voice had lost its compassion and he was confused.

Ken turned the knob and swung the door open, just in time to hear his child asking for a kiss.

"Cuddles?" He turned and looked in my direction. Tears filled his eyes and his face turned red. "Cuddles?"

"Ya, they're all out there, just waiting for you ... Dad."

What took place next could be understood by very few. Ken laughed and cried. He held Cuddles close to his breast and kissed him. He picked up Tweedledee and Tweedledumb and stuffed them in his shirt pockets.

Then he cried again, then laughed. His family had returned and once again, Police Officers had taken a risk to enforce the highest of principles. Clearly, we had broken the law but in doing so, justice was served and the Force's motto "Maintain the Right" was once again upheld.

As I watched Ken hold and pet his birds, I knew our decision was a correct one. Illegal, but correct.

Ken and I laughed together that day. Perhaps, I thought, some day others would know why and understand our motives.

"But I'm still confused," Ken finally managed to ask. "How'd you find them? How'd you get them back?"

"Look, Ken, I just can't tell you. Perhaps some day I'll have the guts to admit what I've done, but it involved a bit of foul play. I had to break the law ... sort of."

"Aren't you worried?" he asked, reminding me of my admission of guilt.

"Naw." I shook my head. "We'll just keep this our secret. Hey, some day the secret will escape but that'll be years from now and then nobody will really care. I've always threatened to write a book y'know. This episode would make a fine chapter."

"Wouldn't that be funny if some day I bought the book and read about Cuddles." He reminded me that Cuddles probably had another 70 years of health and life ahead of him. More than I had.

Shortly after, we loaded the birds, hamsters, rabbits, guinea pigs and snakes back into the store. It was a happy time, punctuated every few minutes by "Ha, ha, ha, give me a kiss, you big white lump."

Cuddles was home.

A few minutes later I climbed into my police car and waved goodbye to Ken and the big white lump that was growing from his shoulder. As I waved I wondered — why do people cry when they're happy?

CHAPTER 9

PEPPER SPRAY

AGE AND TREACHERY
WILL ALWAYS OVERCOME
YOUTH AND SKILL.

It was a good feeling knowing that Constable Schneider and I had just saved a life. In fact we had saved three lives. Bird lives, true, but lives just the same. Long after Birds "R" Us closed and long after Ken Wilson and I had "shuffled off our mortal coils," Cuddles would be around as testament to the value of life. In my mind I could see Cuddles, at the ripe old Cockatoo age of 70, living in a futuristic society, loudly proclaiming, in a voice from the past: "Ha, ha, ha. Give me a kiss, you big white lump."

For the first time in my life I understood why people cry when they are happy. Tears are not only regrets of the past but also hope for the future. Both are a result of great emotion and tears are not always sad.

As happy as I was, however, a voice in the back of my head reminded me that the illegal search could never be disclosed and to do so would mean serious consequences in my career. Another voice, however, reminded me that I did not really care. It suggested that some day when my service and courage afforded me a degree of age, this story could be told with impunity.

"Bravo 6, Surrey." My reverie was interrupted as Sharon's voice called for Stewart over the police radio.

"Bravo 6, Surrey," she called again.

No answer.

Reaching down, I pushed the yellow RTT (Request to Talk) button on my CAD head.

"Go ahead Bravo 23," Sharon answered.

"I think Dudz is still on a hunt, Bev. Can I help?"

"10-4," she replied. "I've got an 'eat-no-pay' at Linton's Pizza Parlor. Can you take it?"

"10-4," I answered. "Put the file in my name. My E.T.A's about four minutes. Any further details?"

"Steve, the owner of the restaurant called. Says he has tried to resolve the matter but has had no luck. Asked for the police to attend."

"Gotcha," I acknowledged. "Any cover cars available?"

"Bravo 23, Bravo 12." Our conversation was interrupted.

"Bravo 23," I answered.

"I'll cover you. My E.T.A. is the same. Meet you out front?"

"10-4," I acknowledged. "Copy Sharon? Constable Wruth is covering."

"Surrey copies. Time dispatched is 1410 hrs.

"Thanks, Sharon. Thanks Bravo 12. See you there." This call did not warrant a Code-3 response. No need for emergency lights or sirens. Disturbances at eating establishments usually meant a drunk was implicated and a certain degree of haste often proved to be helpful.

Constable Ruth had offered to assist with this call. She had been trained by Bev and taught by the best. It was common knowledge that a recruit took on the characteristics of his or her trainer. In fact, the word "clone" had often been used to replace the term "recruit." A trainer and a clone were often as inseparable as a tree and its shadow on a sunny day. For this reason Ruth possessed not only Bev's wisdom and tenacity, but had added one quality of her own — cunning.

In many instances Ruth had developed a reputation for her innovative and downright treacherous moves. She had taken down the biggest drunks with one slap to the ear, stopped many overbearing supervisors with a suggestive wink and dried the eyes of many children with a lollipop which always seemed to appear magically from her shirt pocket.

Perhaps it was her name, Ruth Wruth, that encouraged her resourcefulness. "My parents loved me so much they named me twice," she often said before a witty remark could be made when her name was announced.

Ruth, like Bev, applied her talents to everything she did, every arrest she made and every call she was dispatched to. Although she had just graduated from the Recruit Field Training Program, she had already proved her worth. She was part of our family.

Four minutes later I pulled up behind Ruth's car and radioed our arrival. "Surrey, Bravos 23 and 12 at scene."

"At scene," Sharon acknowledged. "Time is 1415 hours."

Looking ahead I could see Ruth climbing out of her car. She was eager — as usual — to attend any call. A sure sign of youth.

"Well, Bobo, whatchya gonna teach me on this call?" Ruth was a close-enough friend to call me Bobo. In fact, I liked the nickname. It reminded me of the close link we all enjoyed as family members.

82

"Dunno," I answered. "Let's just see what fate has planned for us.

Together we walked through the front door of the restaurant. The smell of tomato sauce made my mouth water. It was well past lunch time and I had not eaten since early morning.

Linton's Pizza Parlor was a small restaurant that survived chiefly on its take-out service. But it also had six small tables and approximately 18 chairs for those who preferred to eat in cramped quarters. Because Linton's was not licensed to serve alcohol, our calls to it were rare.

We had no problem locating the disobedient customer since there was only one patron.

"He's drunk," Steve, the owner, said. "I shouldn't have served him but when he threatened to take this place apart, I thought a quick meal would calm him down. Look, I'm sorry to bother you guys ... uh gal ... uh.... Could you help me out on this, please?" Steve's face blushed when he referred to Ruth as a "guy."

"You're right, Steve," Ruth responded. "You were wrong to serve him, but even knowing that, if you had refused him service, we'd probably have a real mess in here, wouldn't we?"

Steve nodded.

"We'll just see what we can do." She turned to me and smiled. We both knew that Steve was a decent, hard-working man and we wanted to remove his problem as quickly and cleanly as possible.

We walked over to the lone occupant. He had been drinking prior to his arrival at Linton's pizza parlor. The effects of alcohol gave him an aggressive and downright belligerent attitude.

"I'm not gonna pay for this garbage." He looked up at us in defiance.

"Been drinking a bit, have we?" Ruth asked.

"Don't know about you, but I sure have," he admitted, "and if you think you're gonna get me to pay for this crap, I'll shove it so far down your throat they'll call you pepperoni-pants."

"Well, sir, there's no real reason to get upset over a small pizza. Could I just have your name, please."

"Name's Buster," he said. "Buster Head Open if she bothers me any more." The drunk looked at me and winked, then reached for the hot peppers and sprinkled them over his meal.

"Trying to cover up the taste with spice, eh?" Ruth asked.

"Nope, just getting ready to shove it in your face."

"Now, now, no need to be rude, just because you don't like the food." Ruth smiled as she mocked him.

"I'd give all the toes off my right foot for a good pizza," he said.

"All six of them?" Ruth asked.

"Screw you, bitch!" His temper flared.

"We'll be right back," I interrupted, hoping to delay the escalation of hostilities.

I motioned to Ruth and we walked away to neutral territory. I knew Ruth well enough to suspect that she had a plan. She always did. I decided it would best be discussed out of earshot of both Steve and our prisoner-to-be.

"He's over six feet tall and weighs over 240 pounds. We can't take him down without a struggle. Poor Steve'll have the mess-of-a-century to clean up if we try that in here."

"He's a big brute all right," she agreed. "Look, I've got a plan." Ruth unclipped the leather holster which held her pressurized can of pepper spray.

"Oh, no!" I said, trying to keep my voice down. "Not in here. That stuff only blinds them. He'll be like the proverbial bull in a china shop." I did not want to use pepper spray in such confined quarters. Pepper spray worked but it wasn't a remedy which could be liberally applied to all problems.

"Bob, don't you remember what they taught you during pepper spray training?"

I looked at the small red and black canister protruding from Ruth's round, black holster and allowed my mind to drift back a year to the day our instructor introduced us to pepper spray. I could still hear the words:

"Pepper spray, gentlemen. Pepper spray, otherwise known as 'Oleoresin Capsicum.' It is not the great solution you might have hoped for, but it works." Our instructor held out his personal can of RCMP issue pepper spray. "This magic liquid will take most people to their knees in 8-10 seconds." Our instructor, Corporal Joe McNaughton, was nicknamed 'Smokin' Joe.'

Although no one knew exactly how he had earned this reputation, he would often support it with a simple "You haven't seen me angry, have you?" He was a good instructor, though, and held our attention as he spoke. We were all eager to learn the secrets of this elixir which was as effective as a baton, but caused no permanent injury.

"Before we begin the theory portion of this half-day training seminar, we will all proceed outside for a practical demonstration."

Eagerly, 10 police officers filed out the rear door of the police building. All were wondering what unfortunate individual would be stupid enough to volunteer for a "practical demonstration."

"Teather!" Joe called out. "Stand over there." He pointed to

84

the side of the building where a large chalk "X" had been placed on the asphalt. Then he began his address to the class.

"You will likely all have the opportunity to use pepper spray in the next 12 months. So that you will understand exactly what this little canister will do — and will not do and I emphasize 'not' — I will afford you all the opportunity to be the sprayer and the sprayee." He had his back to me and I did not see the wink he gave to the class. "You will also be questioned on its use in court," he continued. "With the experience I will give you today, you will face the judge and explain to him that while debilitating and painful, the discomfort caused by the spray is not inhumane."

"Discomfort?" I shouted out.

"Discomfort!" he said loudly. Then he turned and directed a two-second blast 10 feet through the air. The spray spread as it left the nozzle, each tiny droplet carrying its burning message in my direction.

I could barely feel the spray hit my face and eyes. Amidst the laughter of the trainees, I raised my hand to my face to confirm that I had been hit. My fingers felt moist, yet there was no stinging, no burning.

"The effect of this spray will take approximately 8-10 seconds to be felt by your assailant," instructor Joe called out in a loud voice. "Randal and Robertson, walk over there and help Teather to the decontamination barrel."

"No. I'm okay. I can get there myself, thanks." For the first few seconds I thought our instructor had used the "instructional canister" which contained only water and lanolin oil. I was ready to fake the results.

Faking was not necessary.

I had taken only two steps when the burning launched itself into my eyes in the form of a thousand tiny needles. Small needles at first, then growing to the size of arrows. My eyes were on fire and, against my will, my eyelids slammed shut. The fire spread throughout my eyes and eyelids and they closed even tighter.

"Can everyone see how the veins on this man's forehead are standing out like a road map?" Joe said calmly. "He is in pain. Now we proceed to phase two."

I did not know what phase two was but briefly considered that if it were suicide, it would at very least be merciful.

Joe walked by my side as he continued his lecture. "You should reassure your subject that the pain will not get any worse."

"Can't get any worse if you pop my eyes out with a red-hot poker you bloody...."

85

"And do not be upset with any comments from your subject. They are in considerable pain and...."

"Get me to the bloody barrel or I'll...." I called.

"As I was saying," Joe continued, "reassure your subject."

He placed his hand on my back. "Bob, I know it hurts, been sprayed twice myself. You'll be at the barrel in a couple of seconds, then you can shove your face under the surface of the water and the pain will leave instantly."

"Aaarrrggghhh," I answered. Mercifully, I was led to a large plastic garbage pail full of water. A hose ensured a constant supply of water. My knees hit the garbage pail and I slammed my head down into the water as hard as I could.

"Now open your eyes," Joe said.

Involuntary muscle spasms had sealed my eyelids tight. I briefly raised my head above the water and said, "Can't!"

"You can and you will." Joe pushed my head back into the water. In one great attempt at freedom from the pain, I opened my eyelids.

The pain left instantly.

"You will now notice how your prisoner will enjoy the coolness of the water. How he will enjoy bathing his head in the running water. The pepper spray floats on the surface and will rise away from his eyes. Watch him closely now as he remains calm, enjoying the instant relief the cool water affords."

"Hey, Teather, been down there a long time haven't you? You learning to breath through your ears?"

I was in no mood for humor. I could see the faint green glow of the summer sun shining through the plastic pail. I was in garbage-pail heaven. The problem I faced was that each time I raised my face for another breath of fresh air the burning returned. I was constantly forced to seek the comfort of cold running water.

Joe continued lecturing. "We'll just stay with him for now. In about 20 minutes the pepper spray will be gone and there will be no residual effects."

Twenty minutes later I walked away from the barrel. My eyes still stung slightly and my lips and tongue still burned but the pain had been reduced to the "discomfort" Joe had promised. Apart from that I felt fine.

In the next two hours, all trainees were sprayed. It was not mandatory but we all volunteered. The reason was simple. If anyone complained of the use of this spray we could easily and truthfully give evidence in court that prior to using the pepper spray, we first undertook to comprehend its full impact. We could all look the judge in the eye and say under oath, "Your honor, I have volun-

86

teered to be sprayed. Having been sprayed, I am fully qualified to say that this is a most humane restraint technique. Painfully effective, but humane."

Two hours later, we had all been sprayed, dunked in the decontamination barrel and towelled off. With red welts still adorning our faces, we sat in class for the theory portion of Corporal "Smokin' Joe's" presentation. We listened carefully.

"Oleoresin Capsicum," he explained "O.C. Pepper Spray as we call it, is a safe and efficient method to control an assailant. "It, does not work on individuals who are mentally deranged, high on Angel Dust or those who are highly focused or goal-oriented. This is not a magic panacea, gentlemen. It is, however, the best we have."

"But isn't it harmful, at least to some extent?" Constable Robertson asked. She had been sprayed the worst of us, her face still blotched with large angry-red patches and welts where the pepper spray had landed. Her partner had been most brutal in his attempt to show male dominance. Constable Robertson, however, was clearly braver than any of us. She had spent an extra 15 minutes with her face immersed in the barrel but had not complained. She displayed the qualities of a good cop. Tough and sincere.

"Harmful?" Joe repeated. "Harmful?" We all waited for an answer.

"Oleoresin Capsicum is non-toxic. In fact, it is a food product," he explained, his voice calm but serious. "O.C. spray generates one million Scouville Units of heat. By contrast, a ripe jalapeno pepper generates only 2,000 units. Therefore, O.C. spray is about 500 times more powerful than jalapeno peppers. And," he added, "ain't none of us want even one jalapeno pepper rubbed in our eyes!"

"Food?" Constable Robertson asked.

"Yes, it is," Corporal Joe confirmed. "O.C. pepper spray is actually a food. Want to try some?" The class declined.

"Bob, don't you remember what they taught you during pepper spray training?" Ruth repeated her question and jerked me back to the present — to Steve's restaurant and to our problem.

"Yes." I smiled, looking at Ruth holding her red canister. I now understood her plan.

We walked back to Buster and took up our positions. I stood on his left while Ruth worked her way into a chair on his right. The trap was set and the bait about to be applied.

"Y'know something, Buster?" I knelt down beside the table and closed the distance between our faces. He responded by moving even closer to me — a game of non-physical aggression.

87

"What?" he said. I could feel his hot breath on my face. The odor of alcohol was sickening.

"I'll tell you something, Buster!" I emphasized his alleged name. "I'll bet you can't even eat that little scrawny pizza. That a skinny little fart like you has to pretend it tastes horrible. That you're not the man you pretend to be."

While I lured his attention away from his meal, Ruth added one more topping to his half-eaten pizza. A one-second burst of Oleoresin Capsicum, alias pepper spray, alias a food product.

Steve made the best pizzas in town. Police Officers are adept at locating the best coffee shops, doughnut parlors and pizza restaurants. Experience had told me that this fine pizza had nothing wrong with it — except for the newest topping that Ruth had secretly applied.

"In fact, if you can eat the rest of that pizza in less than five minutes it's yours! Free of charge." I spoke loud enough for Steve to hear. He did not like the offer, but he was not aware of our plan.

"Oh, ya?" Buster shoved the words into my face.

"Oh, ya!" I did likewise. "And if you can't, you will pay full price and leave a nice tip."

"Well, just watch this." The over six foot, 240-pound eating machine picked up the remaining slice of pizza, folded it once and shoved one-third of it into his mouth.

Calmly, Ruth stood up, picked up the large plastic pitcher of ice water that was on the table and slowly walked toward the door.

Buster chewed.

Ruth walked.

Buster chewed.

Ruth smiled.

Buster chewed. His eyes rolled back into his head. For an instant he shuddered. I stood up and increased the distance between us. Buster shook his head from side to side, looked at the table and the missing jug of ice water. Then he opened his mouth wide enough to allow all the food to drop onto his lap.

"HAAARRRGGG." The word came from deep within.

"I beg your pardon?" I said.

"He said HAAARRRGGG," Ruth shouted as she winked at Steve. "Water, anyone?" she offered as she began to walk quickly out the front door to her police car.

"HAAARRRGGG," Buster shouted louder.

Steve looked on. He did not understand what had happened but he knew that whatever Buster had just eaten ... it was HAAAR-RRGGG.

In an instant, the six-foot plus, 240-pound man followed Ruth

88

outside and into her police car. She had placed the pitcher of ice water on the floor in the back seat. Buster eagerly climbed inside and was content to sit still and drink ice water while she closed the door.

"Don't worry, Steve," I called back through the open door. "We'll bring you payment in full and your pitcher in an hour or two."

"Thanks, guys," he said, still wondering what had happened.

Fifteen minutes later I assisted Ruth as she booked in her prisoner.

"Your wallet," she said to him as he continued sipping from the large plastic pitcher, "contains $35, minus $7 for the pizza and $3 rental for the pitcher. Is that okay with you or should I return the pitcher immediately." Buster cradled the pitcher like a baby. A tear ran down his cheek as he feared losing his most prized possession.

"Fine. Hot. Fine. More please?" He held out the pitcher and I showed him the nearby sink. He had become polite and I did not want to take his baby away.

Buster was booked in without further problems. I was completing the report when Ruth returned.

"I'll do that," she said. "You got something to do, don't you?" Ruth knew that my mind was occupied and with a kind nod of her head she sent me on my way.

To Surrey Memorial Hospital.

Fifteen minutes later I pulled up a chair and sat beside Bruce's still unconscious body. His breathing was shallow and his face pale.

"Higgy, it's Bob." I spoke softly. I had heard that unconscious people often hear voices but could not respond. "Higgy," I repeated his name, "I know you can hear me."

I half-lied, half-prayed it was true. "Higgy, you gotta get better. C'mon, Higgy, I know you can open them peepers of yours. It's me, Higgy. Open them eyes." My throat muscles tightened and my eyes blurred with tears. "Please, Higgy, please?"

I talked to Bruce for nearly a half hour. Mostly I just said I was sorry for putting him there. I offered him a lifetime supply of coffee at my expense if he would just open his eyes.

"Higgy, just think of it. Coffee. Coffee for life. I'll even deliver it. Coffee, Higgy. Free coffee for life. Any brand. Any variety. Any size. Please just open them peepers. Please." I begged for a sign of consciousness but there was no response. His hand remained motionless in mine. It was cold and still.

"To hell with the coffee, Higgy. I just want you back. C'mon back, buddy. We need you. Please, Bruce. Please?"

No response.

I had tried everything I knew to rouse my buddy but he remained unconscious. I walked out of the room straight into nurse Jane.

"Does he really like coffee that much?" she asked.

"Ya. Even has his own holder in the police car for his mug. He's a 10 cup-a-day man." I tried to smile.

"The doctors aren't too hopeful right now, Bob. He's just not responding and we don't know why. That's not too bad, though. I've seen many cases like this where they just decide not to open their eyes for a day or two, as if the body just needs time to heal."

"And you've seen times when they don't open their eyes?"

"Yes." Jane spoke honestly as she looked down at the green and black tiles on the floor.

"Here's our dispatcher's private line. Her name's Sharon. Please give us a call if there's any change."

"Sure," Jane said.

I left the hospital and walked back to my car. If there was a way back, Higgy would find it.

He was my friend.

CHAPTER 10

THE GREAT FRASER ISLAND RAID

DEPEND ON A RABBIT'S FOOT
FOR LUCK IF YOU WILL.
BUT REMEMBER –
IT DIDN'T DO MUCH GOOD
FOR THE RABBIT.

As I returned to my police car from the visit with Bruce I watched people coming and going from the Hospital's Emergency Department. The parade seemed like an endless loop in a telephone answering machine tape. A young boy, still crying, was holding his arm as his mother walked with him on their way into the Emergency Ward. As they passed through the doors, another young boy wearing a cast on his arm walked alongside his mother.

"Life's like that. A series of injuries and healing," I thought.

Placing my car in gear I prepared to move out of the parking lot but my way was blocked. In my reverie I had not noticed Bravo 11 pull in front of my car. The white door on Bev's car swung open and she jumped out.

"Hey, guess what? I was talking with Dudz on his cell phone about 20 minutes ago. He says he's got the car! Bloody hell, Bobo, that guy's a miracle maker. He's got a hook on it now and he's having it towed to the Crime Labs. He says the tow truck driver was the one who found the car for him."

"Just like Dudzinski. He puts a whole crew of tow trucks out there to find a crime vehicle."

"And he succeeds dammit, Bobo, he got it!"

"Did you ask him about the suspect?"

"Ya, but he ain't talkin'. Says he'll have him arrested and charged before the party begins at the White House tonight. Wow! What a going away gift for ol' Schlitz. One in custody, gift-wrapped and ready to hang!"

"They don't do that anymore," I reminded Bev.

"It's a shame, isn't it? But I suppose it's not for us to decide. How's Higgy?"

"No change."

"Damn! Hey, did you know that sometimes unconscious people can still hear ... that sometimes if you talk to them they will listen and respond?"

I told Bev of my promise for a lifetime supply of free coffee. My voice trembled as I told her there was no response.

"But maybe he can smell. Maybe if you put a cup of coffee by his bedside," she suggested. "Get that man anywhere near coffee and he's worse than a bloodhound chasing a cheese-ball!"

"Okay, I'll think about it. Spoken to Scooter since this morning?"

"Yes. I just came from her house. She's doing pretty good. Know what, Bobo? Her Dad's coming to town. I spoke to Michelle, her Mom, and she says he even asked if they might get back together. Wouldn't that be a miracle?"

"Yes," I replied. "Sure could use one of those miracles about now."

"Kssshhht. Bravo 11." Bev's radio called her over to the car. She reached for the microphone. "Bravo 11. Clear for a call. Go ahead, Sharon."

"Are you near a telephone?"

"Can be very quickly."

"Give me a landline," Sharon directed.

Our frequency was usually monitored by the news media and criminals. When a confidential communication was necessary, we reverted to the use of a landline — a telephone. Cellular telephones also could easily be monitored, hence the name landline. Direct-wire communication was too difficult to intercept but anything over the airwaves could easily become public knowledge.

Bev walked across the parking lot and disappeared through the Emergency Room doors. I admired her. She was tough as leather and as loving as a mother. As gentle as a kitten but, when threatened, as savage as a lioness. Most of all, though, she was family.

Five minutes later she returned. "Sounds like a good one. Wanna go on a search warrant, Bobo?"

"Stolen property? Drugs? Firearms?"

"Nope," she smiled. "Chickens!"

"Chickens? As in walking, pecking, brown and white barn-yard birds?" I was still puzzled.

"Chickens. As in scratching-the-dirt, waiting to be butchered, Kentucky-fried birds."

92

"What's up?" I asked.

"Follow me to our local Society for the Prevention of Cruelty to Animals. Apparently the SPCA is up to something. I'm not sure but this looks like a good one."

I climbed back into my vehicle still not sure what wondrous plan the future held, but I trusted Bev and she had never taken me on a wild goose — or chicken — chase before. But that voice in the back of my head spoke to me and reminded me of a card which had surfaced in my Deck from time to time:

When choosing between two evils,
always choose the one you've never tried before.

Bev's sideways glance and suppressed smile told me I was about to embark on a new venture. Today had already proved to be unusual. I was eight hours into a 12-hour shift and I had already been involved in an illegal search and a charge of mopery.

The SPCA was a five-minute drive. I followed Bev and together we pulled into the parking lot and exited our cars.

Dogs barking, cats meowing, and other animal sounds met us as we walked across the gravel parking lot to the office. Behind the office, long buildings housed countless stray animals. The lucky ones would soon find homes, the old and sick animals — well, they would soon find peace.

We were all animal lovers on the Watch. Even Denis was rumored to have a pet budgie. It was his wife's, but he was once overheard bragging about its ability to talk. We had even adopted a stray cat and named it C-Watch after our team. We fed it every day and let it sleep in the cellblock on cold winter nights. When it was sick, we all paid the veterinarian bills.

Bev and I spoke lovingly of our stray cat as we walked across the parking lot. We entered the building and were met by the branch supervisor, Brian Wilson.

He was a short man, wore thick glasses and always spoke with a smile. He had taken the job as SPCA Superintendent because he loved animals and wanted to help them. Too many times, though, he guided his charges to a better world through a small needle-prick in the paw.

I never forgot the day he had "put to sleep" two vicious pit bulls seized from a local drug trafficker. After the initial tranquilizer had taken effect, he raised each dog onto the examination table and talked to it in loving terms as he carefully injected a mixture of sodium pentothal and potassium chloride into a vein in their paws. The sodium pentothal drew down a cloak of sleep while the potassium chloride stopped their heart.

93

"Bye, puppy," he said. "You're going to be with friends now. No more need to hate people." Brian would never let us see his face when he completed his "final kindness." Later I was to learn that he cried — alone — in his office, each time he had to say goodbye.

Although Brian loved animals, this time he was angry and motioned us into his office. He closed the door and sat down behind his desk. His face was serious as he opened a manilla file folder and explained the case he was working on.

"Martha Kruntz. We have been watching her for nearly six months and despite all the complaints we have received, she still refuses to comply with our demands."

"What's the problem?" Bev asked.

"Well, she's a bit eccentric — to say the least. Perhaps because she has been living on Fraser Island too long. Who knows? Once you meet Martha, you can make up your mind."

"Get to the point, Brian." Bev cut short his ramblings.

"We went out to her house this morning. She wouldn't answer her door so we did some snooping around. We found a shallow burial pit with the legs and other parts of at least two goats, one horse and a couple other animals sticking out of the mud. We looked behind her house. She has all her cats in tiny travel cages with no water or food and her barn is loaded with chickens and turkeys."

"So what is the problem with a barn full of chickens and turkeys?" I asked.

"They're dead chickens. Well, most of them. There's probably a hundred or so still alive, but in the five minutes I was in the barn, two fell dead from the rafters."

"You got a search warrant signed and ready?" Bev asked.

"Sure do. But that's not why I called you two. Oh, we'll need your help but there's something else you can do for me."

"What's that?" I asked.

"We've been trying to get a court order against Martha for the past two years. No provincial judge will comply. How about pulling a few strings and getting us some media coverage on this one? If anyone can make people feel sorry for a hundred dying chickens and a few turkeys, it's you two." Brian forced a smile.

"Can I use your telephone?" Bev asked.

Brian handed his telephone across the desk. She quickly made a call then hung up. "You know Barry Henley?" Bev asked.

"Sure." Brian's face lit up. "He's a television cameraman. Can you get him to come out on this search?"

Bev laid out her plan. It was a simple one, simple but effective. Barry Henley had been covering a story just south of the Canada-U.S. border on "Canadian impaired drivers in the United

94

States." The courts had closed and he was heading home to bring his story to our local news station. If our timing was good, our plan would succeed.

We all knew that Barry monitored our police frequency; in fact, his timely arrival at many crime scenes had won him several journalism awards. The plan was simple. Stage a broadcast over our police radios that would be irresistible to Barry. In short, hang out the bait and wait for him to bite.

With luck, Barry would arrive on the scene and videotape the search as a human-interest story.

"Just give me a minute, I have one more call to make." Picking up the telephone, Bev called Sharon's direct line in our dispatch office.

"Hi Sharon, it's Bev. I've got a favor to ask of you. Yes ... that's the call we're on ... okay ... we'll be an hour or so on this one ... yes ... I know, it's a shame, all those chickens. Look, Sharon, we're leaving the SPCA office now ... that's right ... I'm ahead of you on this one, Barry Henley is probably at the border crossing now ... okay but just play along with me. I know he monitors our tactical channel but Sergeant Denis never listens to it so whatever I say just play along. Ya, I saw the movie, 'Raid on Entiebbe' — we'll call this 'The Great Raid on Fraser Island.' Thanks, Sharon. Tell the other girls in the radio room to monitor this, we're going to have some fun." Bev hung up and smiled. "How's the six o'clock news for coverage, Brian."

Brian's eyes grew large and he smiled. "I owe you for this."

"Naw," she said. "This ain't exactly by-the-book but I might as well be hung for a lion as a lamb."

As usual, Bev's plans never came from the RCMP Operational Manual, but they were good.

Minutes later, Bev led the parade, which included three SPCA panel vans, on their way to becoming a legend. "West on #10 Highway, then north on 176 Street," she directed over the police radio.

"Bravo 11 and all cars proceeding to Fraser Island, please request if cover is needed." Sharon's voice called out loud over the air. Barry would easily hear this transmission.

"Cover?" I thought. "Cover? We were on our way to seize chickens, dogs and cats. Cover?"

"Surrey, Bravo 11. Request priority on Tact 11 channel please?" Then Bev added loudly to her request. "I repeat. Priority requested for Tact 11. We have an incident here!"

"Priority assigned. All cars attending to Fraser Island please go Tact immediately. Repeat. All cars to Fraser Island go Tact 11

95

immediately and meet Bravo 11. Cars assigned: Bravo 11, 12, 16, and 10."

Ten miles south, at the Peace Arch Border Crossing, Barry Henley leaned forward to adjust his police scanner. He had heard mention of Surrey's Tactical frequency and a list of cars to follow. Something was happening and he wanted to be part of it. Using his cellular telephone he called the television news room and advised his story would be late, but he would be returning with something far more important.

Little did he realize how right he would be!

"Bravo 11 on Tact 11 to all cars. We will meet at the Fraser Island Ferry Landing in 10 minutes. All cars are reminded to dedicate this channel to this take-down and to attend Code 3." In my mind, I could see Bev smile and the girls laughing in the Dispatch Center.

"Bravo 11 and all cars responding," Sharon said next, "please be advised we have E.R.T. activated and they will be on scene shortly."

Wow! E.R.T. What a stroke of genius! Sharon had falsely suggested that our E.R.T. (Emergency Response Team) was being called out. Sharon had already notified the E.R.T. commander of the hoax. He in turn had advised his team not to respond to this request. Barry Henley would be twisting in his seat just listening to the action. He had heard our destination and the importance of our mission. He would head to the chickens immediately upon clearing the border.

The mention of the E.R.T. was perfect. To Barry, it meant Police Officers with black-knit hoods, big assault rifles and camouflage clothing would be on the scene. It meant a sure thing for the evening news. And, news was about to occur. Chicken news!

As planned, all vehicles mustered at the Fraser Island Ferry landing and waited for the small ferry to travel the 100 yards across the Fraser River.

Police officers and SPCA Peace Officers formulated a plan for the raid. It was decided that Bev and Frank would knock on Martha's front door while Rod and I stood by at the back. It was rumored that she had a rifle in her house.

We were not taking any chances. Although it seemed a trivial police operation, we all knew that a big proportion of Police Officers who died in the line of duty were investigating "trivial" incidents.

Our plan was complete. We had only to wait for the ferry. In the quiet, late-afternoon warmth, I allowed my mind to drift back to Regina, Saskatchewan. Back to our graduation. Back to the last

96

words I ever heard Corporal Don Withers speak. It was a speech he gave to our parents and girl friends at our graduation:

"Ladies, Gentlemen and my fellow Police Officers. I have been asked to address you as a group and that is easy because today I am no longer your instructor. I am your equal. You have all volunteered for a most dangerous mission. Police work! In the years to come, some of you will quit the RCMP due to injuries, either physical, emotional or spiritual. I hope these injuries heal with the passing of years." He paused, looked down at the podium, then gazed out over the auditorium. There were no notes on the podium, his downward gaze served only to give him the time to muster the courage to continue.

"I fear also, in time, one or more of you, my Brothers and Sisters, will be killed on duty and for that reason I am happy, yet saddened. I am happy to have known you, every last one of you, to have met your parents and your fiancees. Indeed, it has been my good fortune to be able to call you my Brothers and Sisters." His throat tightened as he continued.

"Yet, for some of us this will be a last goodbye and we know not who or when one of us may be asked to give the ultimate sacrifice. But we know we are all willing to pay that price. You are now all heroes because you have all committed a heroic act. When you were sworn in, you took an oath to protect and to serve — to Maintain the Right of others." Tears decorated a few cheeks in the audience. Girl friends and mothers sniffed as they listened to Don Withers, our most trusted instructor.

"Being sworn-in is an act of heroism. Everything after that is routine. Our citizens expect you all to fulfill your promise and that is a promise I know you all will keep. We have a tradition over 100 years old. A tradition of bravery and honesty. Nothing else."

The room was quiet as Corporal Withers ended his address.

"I wish you all success and a long life, but please remember my words: 'Police work is not inherently dangerous, but it is, however, terribly unforgiving of any degree of carelessness, incapacity or neglect.'"

Then, he leaned closer to the microphone and said softly: "I salute you all — Brothers and Sisters."

I was jerked back to the present by the sight of a dust comet travelling in our direction. The small white van was unquestionably the news cruiser. Barry Henley had taken the bait — hook, line and chicken. Sliding to a halt, he vaulted from his van.

"Hi, guys!" he said, trying to act nonchalantly. Barry knew that monitoring our airwaves for "official news purposes" was strictly against the law. And it got more complicated.

We knew that he knew, and he knew that we knew that he knew. It was all very complex, but there was one common bond amongst us. We trusted Barry and he trusted us. He often video-taped crime scenes for us before taping his news footage and we trusted him enough to allow him access to most of them.

Although everyone knew that Barry came as a result of his intercepting our conversation on Tact 11, he afforded us the courtesy of stating otherwise.

"Just in the area on patrol," he said to Rod. "A confidential source tells me there's a raid on Fraser Island. Mind if I tag along?"

"Sure, Barry. Just follow us."

"Where's E.R.T.?" Barry asked.

"Just follow our directions, Barry. I can only confirm the search warrant and the fact that we are about to take over 100 into custody." Rod looked back at us and winked.

"Over 100! How you gonna transport them? What's the charge? Who is involved? What are the SPCA vans doing here?"

"Pit bulls." Rod said.

"Oh, wow. Thanks, guys. I'll be right behind you."

Seconds later, the ferry pulled up to the loading ramp and the Deck attendant waved us on board. The Fraser Island Ferry was a mutant amongst ferries, composed of a small tug and a barge. They were married with several large cables and served chiefly to transport cars, people and farm machinery to and from the small island.

Carefully, we drove onto the barge, the last two SPCA vans parking diagonally. There was no room for Barry's news cruiser thanks to this creative parking.

"Hey, guys, pull up. I can't get on," Barry called out as the chain was fastened across the stern of the barge.

"Don't worry," Rod shouted back. "The ferry will return for you. Just get off, turn right and drive 'till you see us."

"Okay! Thanks."

With our backs to the news cruiser, we all broke out in laughter. "He's thanking us!" Bev could hardly form the words she was laughing so hard. We joined in.

"Wow!" Brian exclaimed. "We're gonna get supper time coverage on this!"

"Is this really police work?" Frank asked.

Rod turned to his new recruit. His laugh melted to a smile, then disappeared. "Frank," Rod said in a serious voice. "Some day you will understand that this is police work, in its finest form. We may not be catching the world's greatest criminal, but we're righting a wrong and — well, my little friend, just tag along and you'll

98

see. It ain't all shootouts and high-speed chases. God knows I hope you never become involved in a shootout. But, yes, this is police work."

"Teather, bring that ol' Deck of cards here. Got something to show my recruit." I walked over to Rod.

Thumbing through the Deck, he explained its origin to his recruit. "Young feller, this ain't no ordinary Deck of sayings. This is where Corporal Don Withers' soul resides. Teather keeps him imprisoned in his briefcase or pocket usually, but once in a while he lets him out to breath. Here we go now. Read this card:"

Future generations will not judge us
on how we treated ourselves, or each other.
Future generations will judge us on
how we treated our animals.

Pinkewycz read the words slowly. Then he read them again and smiled. "I think I understand," he said. "This is police work."

"You betcha!" Bev called out. She had watched Rod introduce Frank to the Deck. He was being initiated into our family.

A minute later the barge bumped ashore and we filed off the ferry. Tires squealed and red and blue emergency lights were activated briefly. It was all for the benefit of our awaiting newsman.

As clearly choreographed as any play or dance, we pulled into Martha Kruntz's front yard. Bev and Frank ran to the front door, search warrant in hand, while Rod and I quietly ran to the back of the house to prevent her escape should she try to run. Ruth accompanied the SPCA Constables to the barn.

Having made our way around to the rear of the house, we discovered that the back door had long since been nailed shut and the six-foot-high stairs that led up to the door were missing. There was no means of escape at the rear. We returned to the front. In silence, we watched as Frank Pinkewycz learned his first lesson — one never taught at the Academy.

"Open the door, Martha. We have a search warrant," Bev called. But there was no answer. She repeated her call several times. Movement could be heard inside but Martha refused to come to the door.

"Okay, Martha. We'll just leave your copy of the search warrant on the door. We are here to confiscate all your animals. Hear that, Martha? All your animals are being seized." Bev was standing to the side of the door as she spoke but Francis positioned himself directly in front.

"Never stand in front of a door, Frank," Bev cautioned. "That's a good way to catch a shotgun blast!"

"From Martha?" Frank asked.

"From anyone! Don't they teach you guys nothing in the Academy anymore?"

Hardly had she finished her sentence when the door flew open. Martha Kruntz weighed some 200 pounds and filled the doorway. Wearing a see-through nightgown and looking more like a child's large, balloon animal, she screamed, "You bastards got no right here." Then she raised her right leg and caught poor Frank straight between the legs.

"GUK!" Frank's cheeks puffed as he grabbed himself, fell to the ground and rolled over.

"Bitch!" Bev reached out and grabbed Martha by the front of her nightgown and pulled her forward.

"GUK!" Frank repeated as he tried to catch his breath. Martha's body fell beside him.

"You bitch!" Bev repeated her insult then rolled Martha over. "Somebody help me. I can't get her hands to meet," Bev called.

Running over, I knelt on Martha's soft body and handed Bev my cuffs. She linked the pair and cuffed Martha's over-sized wrists.

Frank was not as hurt as we thought. The blow to his manhood had been a glancing one. Disbelief and shock took him to the ground more than the pain. He was already trying to regain his vertical position — and his composure.

"You okay, buddy?" Rod asked.

"I'm okay," a higher-than-normal voice answered. He clearly saw the humor. Frank stood up and brushed the dirt from his pants, being careful all the while not to brush too hard. Although not mortally wounded, Frank would remain sore for a few days.

Reaching down, he rolled Martha on her back and assisted her to a sitting position. "Ouch!" he suddenly exclaimed. "She's got my thumb!"

Looking down, we all began to laugh. Martha had Frank's thumb tightly clamped in her mouth. The creases on her face indicated that she was applying maximum pressure. Frank's plea for help confirmed that, indeed, a problem existed.

"Leave him!" Rod ordered quickly to Bev.

"Huh?" Bev could not believe what Rod was saying. Police Officers never delayed in helping a fallen comrade.

"Leave him!" Rod repeated. "Serves him right! It's about time he learned to get himself out of trouble."

"But...." Bev was interrupted.

"Norma's got no teeth." Rod smiled, then placed his hands on his hips. "Stuck in a bear-trap are we, young feller? Let's see what you can do."

100

We could see the pain that Frank was experiencing but there was no chance of critical injury. He would have to learn to think quickly, though. There was, however, another pain that Frank felt. It was the pain Police Officers feel when they lose control of any situation. Officers take control — they don't lose it.

Frank proved himself in an instant. Reaching down with his left hand, he pinched her nose. She had been struggling and was out of breath. In less than a second she opened her mouth, gasping for air.

"You've been slimed!" Bev looked at the string of drool which still connected Frank to Martha's mouth.

"Enough of this. Load her up in your car. We got work to do." Rod turned and walked to the barn. Quickly, Bev and Frank loaded Martha onto the back seat, closed the door and joined the search party inside the old barn.

It was in an advanced state of decay. Planks were missing from the walls and openings in the roof allowed shafts of light to illuminate the dirty morgue. For a few minutes we stood in silence, allowing our eyes to adjust to the dim light.

Death was everywhere.

Drag marks in the dirt led to the carcasses of two goats which had been heaped in the far corner. A small hole had been dug nearby. As we approached the hole, our flashlights revealed the bodies of countless puppies and kittens.

"Probably new-born." Brian's face was saddened by the sight.

"God!" was all Bev could say as she viewed the pathetic pile. Dozens of tiny furry bodies were heaped together in a shallow grave. Puppies and kittens that were born to curl up in the arms of a child.

All were dead. And everywhere there were chickens and turkeys.

A few chickens still retained enough strength to fly to the rafters but most were on the ground. Still others huddled up to the carcasses of all those who had gone before them.

"Chickens can be cannibalistic," Brian explained. "I see no signs of any feed in this barn, or elsewhere. Likely they have been surviving by eating flesh."

"B-a-a-a-l." A sound unlike anything I had ever heard before came from the opposite corner of the barn. Two young goats were lying, barely conscious, in their own feces. Martha had thrown several shovels full of dirt on top of them in an attempt to bury them. I felt sick.

They were not even dead yet.

"Okay, we have work to do," Brian directed. "We can curse,

swear and cry if you like, but let's save that until we're finished."

"Brian," Rod exclaimed, "we have over 100 chickens, 50 turkeys two sick goats. And have you seen all those dogs and cats in cages behind the house?"

"Of course I have. I was here earlier today."

"How we gonna get them into your vans?"

Brian already had a plan. "You and your rookie can carry the cages and the two poor goats to the van parked on the roadway. Jim will bring his van up to the doorway, then open the side door and lay down the plank I brought."

As the vans were being positioned, we could hear Barry Henley speeding in his news cruiser. Brian looked at his watch, then at Bev. "This is perfect! Just perfect! Bev, you're a master."

Bev left the barn and approached the news van.

"What the...." Barry was confused. "Where's the snipers? Where's E.R.T.? Where's the big bust?"

"You're looking at it, Barry. You wanted news? You got news! How about a human interest story? You owe us that much after all the cases we have invited you on."

Barry Henley surveyed the scene. Officers and farm animals too weak to walk. Cages containing dogs and cats too weak to stand. And chickens everywhere.

"Okay," he said. "Okay. This one ought to do well."

In the next half hour, Barry's videotape recorded sadness, compassion and anger. Police and SPCA officers carrying semi-conscious animals. Talking to them. Telling them they were going to be okay. Meows, near-lifeless barks, clucks and small throaty goat-noises — all made their way onto tape that would reach out and grab the heartstrings of the public.

Barry also videotaped the trail of food that was laid from the barn up the plank into a waiting van and the parade of emaciated, weak chickens eagerly following the food to their new home. His camera recorded other scenes that afternoon. Ankle-deep in feathers, fur and mud, men and women carried pitiful creatures away from hell. The supper-time news would also show the Police Officers' faces lined with anger, disgust and sorrow.

"Could you tell me more about this raid?" Barry asked as he pointed his lens directly at Ruth's face.

"Not now." She turned away quickly before her tears were made public. Ruth was holding the lifeless body of a kitten which had just died in her arms. To all of us, what had began as a fun event turned into a horribly sad affair.

Barry videotaped Ruth as she stooped to pick up a chicken. "He's still alive!" she called.

Then, halfway to the van, she stopped. Ruth looked down at the thin feathered bird and wept as she placed his lifeless body on the ground beside her kitten. At first we invited the intrusion of videotape onto our activities, then as the scope of the hell became understood, we felt as if Barry's lens was intruding on something personal. Horribly personal. But as the search concluded, we once again welcomed his presence. Barry's efforts would graphically, sadly, show the public what had happened on Fraser Island that day.

When all animals had been loaded, we grouped together for a short debriefing. Our newsman was invited.

Kruntz will be lodged in cells and charged with cruelty to animals. She will be released from jail, likely early tomorrow. We will press for a speedy trial and likely she will be given only a slap on the wrist by the Provincial Court judge. The SPCA will make application for forfeiture of all the animals and an additional application to prohibit her from owning any animals for five years.

"What will you do with all these animals?" Barry's voice projected itself from behind the camera.

"They will all receive veterinary care and be given to people who will care for them."

"Even the chickens?"

"Even the chickens," Brian replied. "I'm not sure how we'll do this, but I promised every dog, cat, goat and chicken a happy home." As he finished speaking, the camera turned to the side and recorded Frank, limping slightly, speaking to Rod.

"I see what you mean," he said, smiling. "This is police work."

That night the supper-time news hour aired the entire story. It was a story of dogs, cats, goats and chickens — and a story of hope.

Martha Kruntz appeared in court three months later. She was given a suspended sentence and barred from owning animals for five years. The animals were awarded to the care of the SPCA.

The same week Barry Henley arranged a follow-up, human-interest story. Videotaped at the local SPCA office, it showed goats, dogs and cats being ushered out by smiling people who promised to care for their new pets.

Amidst the parade of new pet owners, one small blond-haired boy half-sniffled, half-cried as his father left the office carrying two chickens. I will never forget the young lad's words:

"But, Daddy, I wanted a puppy!"

CHAPTER 11

HIS HEAD EXPLODED

I CAN NEVER UNDERSTAND YOUR PAIN
BUT, HAVING CRIED,
I CAN UNDERSTAND TEARS.

As we left Fraser Island we all shared the same emotions — anger and sadness. Even Barry had been deeply affected by what he saw. Nothing would ever erase our feelings or the memories we shared, but the life of a Police Officer is often a unique amassing of emotions, stronger emotions replacing weaker ones until they all jumbled together.

Our next call was to compound the sadness left over from Martha's barn. It was the sort of call that all Police Officers fear — the type of call that sometimes results in the loss of life. It involved a gun and a mentally ill subject. A deadly mix.

Sharon's voice broke the silence. "Surrey, Bravo 16, we have a priority domestic dispute." She sounded very serious.

"Surrey, Bravo 16." She again called Rod and his recruit.

"Go ahead, Sharon," Rod replied.

"Domestic dispute between mother and 16-year-old son. Location is 17695 Maple Drive. Stop check." Sharon temporarily ended her transmission to ensure the information was copied accurately.

"17695 Maple Drive," Rod confirmed.

"10-4," Sharon answered. "Complainant's name is Dexter, I spell, Delta, Echo, X-ray, Tango, Echo, Romeo. Given one, Wanda. Her son, Terry, is apparently out of control. Info I have is he has not been taking his medication ... has been diagnosed as schizophrenic ... caution flag shows there are firearms in the house. Repeat ... firearms in the house. Complainant states her son is threatening to shoot himself. Complainant states she will meet you outside the residence."

"10-4," Rod acknowledged. "We'll be there in five.

"Time out is 1630 hrs. Car to cover, please?"

I reached down and pushed the yellow DTL button. My car radio would now send a message to the communication center detailing my car to this file.

104

"Bravo 23 copy. Bravo 12, also copy." Ruth had also pushed her Detail button and would be covering this call.

"Bravo 23 and 12 have Rod in sight. Will be arriving together." I could still see Rod's car and a quick check in my rear view mirror showed Ruth was behind me. We would arrive as a team.

I hated guns. Even the one I wore. Guns meant injury or death. Police Officers never use a gun as a threat, if the gun is drawn, the Police Officer is ready to shoot. This call might mean a death.

My guts twisted.

Police Officers are often called upon to be more than one person. As I accelerated to the scene a part of me drove the car while my other part detached itself and travelled back in time to the Police Academy, to advice given by a trusted friend one cold winter night.

The memories superimposed themselves on the windshield of my police car:

Regina, Saskatchewan. December.

I stood on the side of the parade square of the RCMP Training Academy. Corporal Don Withers had just threatened me with expulsion from the Academy if I could not lift the mandatory 125 pounds of steel over my head. Amidst the cheers of my troopmates and threats from Corporal Withers, I managed to lift 145 pounds of iron that night. Withers had taught me that even anger, if directed and controlled, could be an asset.

"Know what this is?" He pointed to a cairn five feet from where we stood. On it were names of Mounties who had died in the line of duty. Brave Mounties, all.

"Yes, Don. I do." In private he had allowed a few of us to address him by his first name. "They are our Brothers who have given the ultimate sacrifice. They have upheld their oath. But there's so many of them."

Corporal Withers' face lost all expression. To this day I am not sure if it was my words, or the faint light from the winter stars reflecting off the snow, but a death-like mask covered his face.

"So many of them. Yes, my young friend ... so many." He did not move as he looked at the memorial cairn.

"Do you have any idea what this monument represents? Did anyone ever teach you how many of your Brothers and Sisters have died in the line of duty since the birth of the Royal Canadian Mounted Police?

I looked at the cairn. It was a small monument. "Ten?" I asked. His head moved side to side. "Twenty?" No response. "Fifty?" I knew we had not lost more than 50 members of our

Force. If we had lost 50 Police Officers, I was sure that our academic instruction would cover such a serious topic.

"Fifty?" I repeated.

"No." Don bowed his head. "376."

"376?" I asked, repeating the number.

"Yes," he repeated in a voice almost too soft to hear. "376."

"It's such a small cairn," I said, looking at the tiny memory of 376 souls who had gone before.

"Perhaps one day people will know how police work damages a person's soul," Don said. "Some day, somewhere, someone will have the courage to speak out and tell the public that our line of work carries with it an uncommon danger." Then he looked up in my direction. "But until that day, our Force will just hold that tiny secret, locked safely in some file drawer for no one to see, for no one to remember."

"Why, Don? Why so many? Were they shot? Knifed? Beaten to death?"

"No," he said. "Most of them died because they just did not know how to face adversity. Some of them drank too much and drove their police cars into the water; some paddled a canoe out into rough water, trying to rescue a boater in distress and not taking the time to put on a life vest; some ran out onto thin ice, only to smash through and drown with their would-be rescuee. You see, we're all walking on this sheet of ice. Physically, emotionally and spiritually we're all on thin ice and ... some of us will break through."

It was hard for my young mind to comprehend the depth of this conversation, but Corporal Withers persisted.

"The day after you graduate from this fine establishment," he held his arms outstretched, mocking the Academy, "you will be walking on thin ice. Don't fall through!" He raised his voice. "You see that Deck of cards I gave you?"

"Yes." I still held them firmly in my right hand.

"Well?" He tapped the Deck.

Shuffle. Cut. Turn over top card:

For those who fight to preserve it —
life takes on a meaning the protected
will never know.

"You must be prepared at all times to protect your life and those of others. Many Officers die when they are trying to protect another person. Their death is noble — but it is also final." Then he added. "Keep your mind 60 seconds ahead of your body. Prepare. Anticipate."

106

"Prepare. Anticipate." I spoke the words out loud as we neared the address. "Thanks, Don." The memory was once again part of my conscious mind. I planned to remember the words that Don Withers had taught me.

"Bravos 16, 12 and 23, at scene," Rod's voice called over the radio as we drove up to the house.

Stopping our cars 200 feet from the house, we stood behind mine to formulate a plan. When firearms were involved or even suspected, police never parked in front of the perpetrator's residence. Our purpose was to locate and disarm the offender, not act as an easy target.

"There's Wanda now." Rod pointed to a middle-aged woman walking our way. "I've been here before. Her son's crazy. Poor woman. If she could only keep him on his medication."

"Help!" she called as she ran to our cars.

Her story was familiar. We had heard it before at countless different houses. Terry was 16 years old. He had been diagnosed as schizophrenic three years ago and was doing well when he was on his medication. Most of us knew her son. We had been at their house many times for minor disturbances and we had developed a friendship for this family.

It was not their fault that such an affliction should find their home. It was not their son's fault that he heard voices directing him to hide under his bed for two days and to stop eating for a week. Nor was it Wanda's fault that she had cried herself to sleep most nights, wondering if this affliction would take her sanity. She loved her son but did not know how to control his disease.

Through many visits, we had all come to know Terry and we felt sorry for him, but there was nothing we could do. He was not usually violent. His illness most commonly shoved him into the corner of a room — scared. Carefully, we would speak to him and help him understand that the voices he heard were not real. Poor Terry was a nice young lad.

But his disease was a curse that no one understood. And it was the curse that threatened to kill him — and perhaps others.

The drugs he had been prescribed kept most of the voices away and allowed him to see through the fog that the illness had pulled down. But there was a difference this time.

He had a gun.

"Where is he now?" Rod asked.

"He's locked in the master bedroom."

"Where is that?"

"It overlooks the back yard. There is a small balcony which overlooks the yard but it is about eight feet up from the ground.

107

I've been talking with him for over an hour. I'm scared." She began to shake all over. "He's found my husband's hunting rifle and the bullets. Says he's going to save the world. He's going to shoot the Devil."

"Not good," Rod said. "The Devil will likely be the first person to walk through the door. Do you have a telephone in the bedroom?"

"Yes, but he's ripped the wire out of the wall. He says the Devil uses the telephone to talk to him."

"We got a problem here." Rod was serious. "I'd like to call out E.R.T. and a negotiator but Denis will likely make my life miserable because of the overtime. Suggestions?"

We remained silent.

Rod was the senior officer. It was his duty to formulate a plan, review it with us, then lead the way. It did not take him long. In less than a minute we had our orders.

"Ruth, you take the back of the house. Find a position where you won't get caught in the crossfire." He turned to Mrs. Dexter. "Don't worry, Mrs. Dexter, we won't shoot. We're just worried about your son shooting at us."

Realizing he had already said too much, he offered her a seat in the rear of his police car and closed the door. He did not tell her that there were no inside door handles. She was secure for now. We could implement our plan without her interference.

"Ruth, you got the back of the house," Rod repeated his directions. "Frank, you and I will make first contact and Bob, you back us up. He has to come through the bedroom door or out the patio if he wants to escape. We'll cover both exits. Ruth, if he bails out over the balcony and he still has the gun with him...."

"I understand." Ruth accepted the responsibility. We could not allow him the advantage of mobility. It was the first rule of Hostage Barricaded-Persons negotiations. As long as Terry was contained, we controlled the situation and could prevent further escalation.

Control. That was our prime objective. Control and diffuse.

If Terry decided to jump from the balcony, gun in hand, Ruth would have to shoot him. There was no polite way to describe her duty. She could not allow him to escape into the neighborhood where he might find another Devil to shoot, nor could she allow him the courtesy of having the first shot at her. Dexter forfeited his right to freedom when he picked up the loaded gun. He would forfeit his life if he attempted escape.

"Surrey, Bravo 16 on portable." Rod held his portable close to his mouth.

"Bravo 16," Sharon responded.

"We're switching to Tact 11."

108

"10-4." Rod spoke in a quiet and routine voice, hoping that Barry would still be homeward bound with thoughts of chickens and goats. We trusted Barry but had no time for him now.

We were scared. Bloody scared.

"I gotta pee." Ruth's face was red with embarrassment.

"In your pants, lady," Rod said sharply. We had no time for the luxury of a toilet break. Ruth knew that and so did we. There are few professions in this modern world which require you to dodge bullets, drive a fast car, wear a gun, rescue chickens and pee your pants.

We were indeed, special people.

Rod resumed explaining the plan. "Ruth, get into position. We'll enter through the front door and walk up the stairs to the second level. We'll stay back until you give us the go-ahead."

Ruth ran along the cedar hedge and turned down the driveway. Rod opened the front door carefully as he knelt, offering as small a silhouette as possible in case Terry had walked downstairs.

"Front room clear." Rod spoke softly over his shoulder. Frank followed close behind Rod and I trailed five feet behind them.

"In position." Ruth's voice came calmly over the portable radio.

"10-4 Ruthy-baby," Rod called back. "We're goin' upstairs now. Heads up, Kiddo!"

Rod knew we were tense and tried to ease our adrenaline rush with his own version of on-site humor. "Stay close, Frank. Walk softly. We'll make a Ninja out of you yet."

Without a sound, they climbed the stairs and walked to the bedroom door. I followed about 10 feet behind.

"I'm knocking on the door." Rod spoke into his portable to alert Ruth in the event Terry bolted from the balcony.

"10-4," Ruth acknowledged.

Rod reached out and tapped lightly on the bedroom door with the back of his hand. He wanted to put as much distance as possible between himself and the bedroom door. A bullet fired through the door would be much better discharged into thin air than Rod's stomach.

"Who is it?" Terry called.

Rod turned to Frank and said, "This is good, Frank. At least he's talking to us."

"Terry, it's the RCMP."

BANG!

A hole exploded in the door as Terry fired his first shot.

"This is not good, Frank," Rod said, not taking his eyes from the hole in the hollow core door. "But at least I can see inside."

"Shots fired!" Using her portable radio Ruth alerted all cars in the area.

"Belay that. Cancel. Cancel. Cancel." Rod corrected her as he

109

spoke into his portable radio. "I repeat. Cancel that last transmission."

Rod did not want sirens to escalate the already loss of control he had over the situation. Words were still his best weapon. Sirens would undo any calmness he could project into the bedroom. "Cool it, Ruthy," Rod calmly advised. "We're okay. Just keep your skin tight!"

"Terry?" Rod called. "Good shot, buddy. You bagged yourself a door. Now how's about putting down your Dad's hunting rifle and talking this over with us?"

No answer.

"Yo, Terry. My name is Rod. I'm with the RCMP. Let's talk this over, buddy."

"You the Devil?" Terry asked.

"Nope."

"You sent here by the Devil?"

"Nope."

"What do you want?"

"Just to talk."

"You're the Devil," Terry screamed. "You've been talking to me all week."

"No, Terry. I'm not the Devil. How can I prove that to you?" Even with the closed door separating them, Rod was now entering into a face-to-face negotiation. It was the most dangerous and least recommended category of negotiation — and the least successful. Face-to-face negotiations allowed for emotions to escalate too quickly. It afforded no safety for the negotiator and it gave the barricaded person a sense of impending attack.

Face-to-face negotiations are often forced upon Police Officers who are controlled by restrictions such as supervisors with small minds, and large budgets with small emergency allocations. Rod would have preferred to call in the Emergency Response Team with their negotiators. But had he insisted, he would suffer the consequences. Modern police managers were all too often more engrossed in budget allocations and finances than they were in protecting the public and serving their fellow Officers.

Rod was trapped.

Terry was trapped.

The next move was to be guided by fate.

"Visitor! We have a visitor!" Ruth called over her portable radio. In our absence, Wanda had crawled over the front seat of Rod's car and made her exit from a front door because Rod's car was still equipped with an out-of-date prisoner shield. Budget restraints would not allow his car to be equipped appropriately for another two years.

110

"Say what?" Rod called back.

"It's Mrs. Dexter," Ruth whispered over her portable. "She's here with me."

"Hold onto her, Ruth." Rod holstered his portable radio and sat down.

"Damn!" he said. "Damn. Damn. Damn."

"What's the problem?" Frank asked.

"Shut up, I'm thinking," Rod snapped back. Then he began to think out loud. "Let's see now ... puts a whole new light on this doesn't it, Roddy!" He spoke to himself. "If Terry knows his Mom is in the backyard, he'll put on quite a show, won't he. If he thinks he's alone, he just has me to talk to and he has nothing to prove to me. Damn. Damn." Rod continued speaking out loud, partly to collect his thoughts and partly to keep Frank up-to-date with his plans.

"This is not good, Frank. Not good at all. We have to divert Terry's attention. Can't let him know his Mom's in the yard." Frank nodded, not completely understanding what was happening but silently listening, awaiting instructions.

"Terry!" Rod called out loudly, then softly spoke into his microphone. "Ruth, get her the hell out of there. Now!" He knew that Terry would answer his call and, while speaking, would not hear Rod whisper into his radio.

"Yes?"

"Terry. We gotta talk! Please? I'm asking, please, Terry? The Devil don't ever say please, does he?"

SLAM!

Terry had flung open the bedroom door. Pointing the gun towards the open door, he then slowly walked backwards toward the open patio window.

Things were heating up now.

I had to pee.

Rod inched forward, keeping low to the floor. He did not know if Ruth could control Terry's mother and had to act fast.

"Terry — No!" Rod had made eye contact with Terry. Quickly, Frank and I impulsively took up defensive positions. No training, no theory, just instincts.

Frank moved two feet closer to Rod. They were in the doorway, crouching. Guns were drawn and pointed.

The stage was set, the curtains were drawn and the actors were about to play their final roles.

Time dilated. The seconds slowed to minutes as the final performance was executed.

Terry Dexter slowly walked backwards through the open glass patio window and stood on the patio. His back was against the railing.

Rod's instincts told him what was happening and he tried to stop it.

"Terry, no!" In slow motion, Rod raised his hands, palms outstretched and fingers pointing to the ceiling. With all his authority, he was attempting to stop Terry.

"No! Terry. No!" Rod called again as I took my position behind and to his left.

It was as if a slow-motion movie was projected on a screen and we were invited as viewers. We had ceased being participants.

Terry stood on the balcony. Rod remained crouched in the bedroom doorway. Holding the .303 caliber rifle waist high, Terry fired. Rod, Frank and I heard the loud crack from the rifle and then the "Zeeeee" as the bullet passed by our ears and through the wall behind us.

Few people have ever heard a bullet fired so close to their heads. It is a sound that lingers a lifetime.

As the shot was fired, Rod had called out. He should have shot Terry where he stood, but Rod valued human life — all life — above his own.

Together, we were held prisoners in a slow-motion movie. We watched as Terry called out for deliverance. He swung the rifle around and placed the muzzle in his mouth.

"No!" Rod whispered. His loud calls had failed to command Terry's attention. A whisper might prove effective.

"No," Rod said even softer.

Terry's eyes focused on us as he pulled the trigger.

The bullet entered his head through the roof of his mouth and exited through the top. Most of his skull and its contents were blown some 100 feet in the air, but a portion sprayed forward, off the ceiling and onto Rod and Frank.

"No," Rod called again, hoping to reverse the time line and restore life to Terry.

In the same second that Terry's life left his body, the force of the bullet catapulted him over the wrought iron railing and down onto the grass.

His mother screamed.

Terry was dead. He had died the instant the bullet entered his head, but the medulla portion of his brain still sent out signals to his muscles. He lay twitching on the grass. It could just as easily have been one of us.

Terry's mother held his body and sobbed while she asked the question to which mankind has never been given an answer. "Why, Oh, God. Why?"

We had run to the balcony in time to see Ruth kneeling beside Terry's body. She placed her arm around Wanda and held her as she cried.

112

"Surrey, Bravo 16, on portable," Rod called.

"Bravo 16."

"We have shots fired, no Police Officers down. It's a suicide, Sharon. He bloody-well shot himself." Rod released the button on his microphone, took a deep breath and regained control. "Advise Sergeant Denis please. We'll also need the coroner and E.H.S., A.S.A.P." Rod had called for Emergency Health Services, an ambulance and the coroner. Recent policy, generated by Headquarters, forbid us from pronouncing death prior to moving the body, except in cases of complete decapitation. Poor Terry still retained a portion of his head.

Because of policy set in some bureaucratic office, Terry's body would have to lie on the grass for over an hour before being removed. The reason was simple — bureaucrats had decided that Police Officers did not possess the knowledge necessary to presume death.

We turned and then joined Ruth who still held her arm around Wanda Dexter.

Ruth would not try to force Wanda away from her son's body. She allowed her time to cry, time to ask the question to which there was no answer, and time to cry again.

One hour and fifteen minutes later, Terry's body would be pronounced dead by a doctor who maintained a distance of 15 feet. I gazed at Terry's lifeless shell and felt sad. All his hopes, memories, dreams — all that he was and ever could be, was about to be carefully placed on a metal stretcher and taken away.

His torment was over.

Frank stood beside Rod, shaking. Not a word had been said as they both looked at Terry's body. Then Rod turned to his new recruit, "It's okay Frank. We did the best we could. Some days you win ... some days you lose."

"But we could've...."

"Stop it!" Rod spoke the words clearly. "Stop it! You wanna feel guilty, pick some other place, some other time. Not here! This ain't your fault. It's, It's...." Rod faltered, then said, "The Devil made him do it."

Frank nodded, then looked back at Terry's body.

Later, as I walked toward my police car I passed close by Rod and Frank as they sat in theirs. Frank was still shaken. Badly. And Rod just looked ahead, through the windshield of his car, expressionless. As I walked by I heard him say, "His head exploded, Frank. His head exploded."

We would all deal with today in our own way. But the pain remained. For all of us.

CHAPTER 12

REVENGE DENIED

*TO KNOW WHO YOU ARE
AND WHERE YOU ARE GOING
IS BUT THE FIRST STEP
OF YOUR JOURNEY.*

I walked into the police station staring straight ahead. Details of our stand off with Terry Dexter had preceded us and eyes turned away as I walked down the corridor.

There is a great wall which separates the living and the non-living. I had stood too close to death. I knew that for several days those who worked at the office would feel uncomfortable around me. For the next few days, Rod, Frank, Ruth and I would be alone.

I was shaken by the experience and felt every emotion possible, bidding for space inside my heart and my head.

Anger wanted to speak for the way Terry had treated us.

Sorrow also wanted its turn to let me express how sad I was, seeing a young man needlessly end his life.

And confusion — confusion took all the other emotions, jumbled them together and left me wondering why I had ever chosen to become a cop.

Behind me, Rod, Frank and Ruth followed. No one spoke to us. They did not know what to say. Prior to our arrival, every Police Officer, every stenographer, every person in the building had been briefed on Terry's death. Because no one knew what to say, or how to say it to us, they said nothing.

Sitting in the Constables' office, I pulled out the necessary forms which all of us would have to complete prior to going off shift. Pink forms for the coroner. Green forms for exhibits such as the rifle and the lead slug we carved from the wall. More green forms for the film we would send off to our Headquarters in Ottawa for developing. Green and white forms for the police report. Black and white forms for the telex that would be sent to our Headquarters in Vancouver. Blank paper for statements. We would all write statements. Statements that would likely be read by many, but understood by few.

Paperwork!

All Policemen hate paperwork. It did serve its purpose, however. For the next hour we would be so busy filling out forms, sending telexes, and writing statements that the pain we felt would be shoved aside.

Rod walked in and sat down beside me. Frank and Ruth had disappeared into the locker room to wash and put on fresh clothes. They all carried Terry's blood on their clothes as a silent reminder of his sad and untimely death.

Rod sat motionless. Silent.

I shoved the forms aside and looked at my old friend.

"You okay, Rod?" It was a stupid question. I knew he was not okay but I had to ask.

No answer.

"You okay, buddy?" I repeated the question.

"His head exploded, Bob. His bloody head exploded. He just shoves the barrel into his mouth and pop! His bloody head exploded. I got Terry all over me. Look!" Rod picked a couple of pieces of red-stained bone from the front of his shirt. Blood speckles had dried on his face and he wore part of Terry on his hands. "Bone! Blood! His head just exploded." Rod's face showed no emotion. He was in shock. He turned to me for a brief second, then buried his face in his hands.

"His head just bloody-well exploded."

I reached over and put my arm on Rod's shoulder. I did not interfere. I did not tell him everything would be okay and I did not tell him I understood.

Pain is something that Police Officers cannot truly share. We witness each other's pain. We accompany each other through our pain and we hold each other through the worst part.

But we do not share it. Pain is a private event for a Police Officer. If he is to survive, he must learn how to deal with it in his or her own unique way.

There is no book written and no mental health professional that can give directions on how to survive an exploding head.

I did what I had to do. Knowing Rod was sinking deep into his own pain, I used his courage to pull him out. Rod would put his pain aside if he thought another person needed his help.

"What about Frank. It's his first suicide. How are you gonna help him through it, Rod?"

Rod looked up, dried his tears and spoke. "Well, I'll tell ya' what we're gonna do. It ain't in the books and I don't know if it's right, but I'll tell ya." Rod regained his self-control. "We're going to ol' Schlitz's party tonight. We're gonna wish him well and we're gonna' pretend this never happened. Then after the party ... when everyone else has gone home...." Rod's voice cracked. "Me and Frank are gonna' get drunk. When Frank and I are too drunk to care anymore, we're gonna cry this thing out. Then we're gonna have another drink and go to sleep. That's our bedroom for tonight." Rod pointed in the direction of the White House. "Then after we sleep the night through, we'll wake up about noon, shower, shave and report for night shift. Then we're gonna go out there and do some police work."

Rod had self-prescribed a remedy that worked, although it was not a good remedy. Like any self-prescribed remedy, it held its own dangers. If this medication was taken too many times, it became destructive. Liquor would help dull the pain and displace it. Pain, even the great pain that Rod felt, taken in small doses can be handled. Rod and Frank would drink to kill the pain. The following day, their headache would also help displace the pain of today's injury and a few days from now they would recover.

Unfortunately, this remedy took casualties.

Too many good cops lost themselves in the warm, seductive arms of a bottle of liquor. They retired — often divorced, alcoholics, not knowing how it all began.

"Take it easy on Frank, Rod. He's still a puppy," I said.

"Take it easy on him?" Rod raised his voice. "He's wearing part of Terry on his shirt, his hands and his face! Take it easy on him? His second day at work and we pull the old 'exploding head' trick on him! Take it easy on him, I...."

"Hi, guys." Ruth and Frank entered the room. Rod regained his dignity and self-control.

"How you guys doin'?" He asked the same question I had asked him two minutes earlier.

"I'm okay," Ruth lied. "But Frank's a bit shaky," she added, looking at Frank's pale face.

"Well, we got us a heap of paper work to do," Rod said. "Frank, why don't you take that bullet you got in your pocket, the one you dug from the wall, and fill in the exhibit report."

Frank pulled the deformed lead slug from his pocket. He did not change his shirt, like Ruth he only washed. As he looked at the bullet, his eyes trailed up his arm and across his upper chest. The blood spatter threw him back in time and the pain resurfaced.

"God in Heaven." He shook all over. "Look at me. I wanted to help people ... now I'm wearin' them. I got Terry all over me. Look at this Rod. Little bits of Terry all over me. What the hell am I

116

doing here? Hell, I don't even know who I am anymore and it's only been two days. I didn't sign up for this. I wanted to be a cop."

Rod stood up and looked eye-to-eye at his recruit. Snapping his fingers, he held his hand out in my direction. "Deck!" I unbuttoned my shirt pocket and unwrapped the Deck.

"See this?" Rod held it out then stuck it into his shirt pocket. "Teather ain't getting it back, not tonight he ain't. Later, after ol' Schlitz's party is over, you and me are gonna read this thing together. One by one. I'm gonna tell you about a great man called Withers and you're gonna listen. You say you didn't join the RCMP to do this? You wanted to help people? What the hell do you think would've happened if we had let Terry escape with his gun? You don't really know what it's all about, do you Frank!"

Frank remained quiet and nodded his head side-to-side.

"You don't really know what the hell a Police Officer is, do you Frank?"

He shook his head again.

"Well, I'll tell you what the hell a Police Officer is. It's written on one of these little cards that Teather let me read a long time ago. I memorized it and you will memorize it tonight when we read it together!" Rod had raised his voice. Knowing that what was to come would be a private affair, Ruth walked over and closed the door.

No visitors allowed.

"I'll tell you what a Police Officer is, Frank, and you just listen!"

Rod drew a deep breath and in a staccato voice he began. "Policemen are human, believe it or not — just like the rest of the population. They also come in various sizes and shapes, depending on whether you are looking for one or trying to hide something.

"Policemen are found everywhere — on land, on the sea, in the air, on horses, in cars and sometimes in your hair. In spite of the fact that 'you can't find one when you want one,' they are usually there when it counts the most. The best way to get one is to pick up the phone!

"Police Officers deliver lectures, babies and bad news. They are required to have the wisdom of Solomon, the disposition of a lamb, muscles of steel and are often accused of having a heart to match. We are the ones who ring the doorbell, swallow hard and announce the passing of a loved one. Then spend the rest of the day wondering why we ever took such a crummy job.

"On television, a Police Officer is an oaf who couldn't find a bull fiddle in a telephone booth. In real life he's expected to find a 'little blonde boy, about so high' in a crowd of a million strangers.

117

In fiction, he gets help from private eyes, reporters and 'who-dun-it' fans. In real life, mostly all he gets from the public is, 'I didn't see nuttin.'

"When we serve a summons, we're a monster. If we let you go, we're a saint. To little kids we're either a friend or a bogey-man, depending on how the parents feel about us. We work around the clock, split shifts, Sundays and holidays and it always kills us when some joker says, 'Hey, tomorrow is a holiday. I'm off. Let's go fishing.' That's the day we work 20 hours.

"A policeman is like the little girl who, when she was good, was very very good, but when she was bad, she was horrid. When a Police Officer is good, 'he's on the take - and that goes for the rest of them too!' When he shoots a hold-up man, he's a hero, except when the asshole is only a kid. Then 'anybody coulda' seen that!'

"Lots of cops have homes, some of them covered with ivy, but most of them covered with mortgages. When he drives a big car, he's a chiseler! A little car and 'who's he kidding?' A cop's credit is good. That is helpful because his salary isn't.

"A policeman sees more misery, bloodshed, trouble and sunrises than anyone else. Like the postman, the policeman must be out in all kinds of weather. His uniform changes with the season or climate, but his outlook on life remains about the same — mostly a blank, but hoping for a better world.

"Policemen like days off, vacations and coffee. They don't like car horns, family fights and anonymous letter writers. They have unions but they can't strike. They must be impartial, courteous and always remember the slogan, 'At your service, to protect and to serve.' This is often hard, especially when some goofball reminds him, 'I'm a taxpayer. I pay your salary.'

"Police Officers get medals for saving lives, disarming criminals and shooting it out with bandits. Sometimes, their widow gets the medal.

"But once in a while, the most rewarding moment comes when, after some small kindness to an older person, he feels a warm handclasp, looks into the grateful eyes and hearts of a wrinkled face and hears the words 'Thank you and God bless you — you have helped'."

Rod drew a slow, long breath and softly added, "That's what a Police Officer is, Frank. That's who we are. That's what we do. Can you understand that?"

Franks eyes had filled with tears, yet he said nothing.

Rod took two steps toward Frank and embraced him. Ruth and I stood up and quietly left the room. Closing the door softly

118

behind us, we heard Rod speak the words, "It's okay, Brother. It's okay. We'll be okay."

"Good ol' Roddy," Ruth said softly. "Sure knows what to say and how to say it."

I did not reply. She was right. Rod had long ago learned that the best way to keep your strength was to give it to others.

Rod was a master. He was our friend.

Together, Ruth and I stood in the hallway. We pushed the world aside for a brief moment and privately shared our feelings, thoughts and prayers that tomorrow would be a better day and....

"Cellblock! Cellblock! Cellblock! Member to the Cellblock, please!" The office public address system called. It could mean only one thing. Our guards were retired men, ex-military and policemen. Their age precluded them from any physical confrontation. At the sign of any problems, they pushed the button on a wireless transmitter they carried.

The announcement meant a serious problem existed in the cellblock and immediate assistance was required.

Bev and I ran down the hall, turned left and hit Sergeant Denis a glancing blow. Ricocheting off the walls, the three of us headed straight for the cellblock door.

"Damn," Sergeant Denis suddenly said. "Left my key in the office." He had committed a major error. He was required by policy to have the key on his person at all times. Ruth, however, never followed policy. Drawing a large lock-knife from an "unapproved" holster on her gunbelt, she slid the blade between the door and the jam. The bolt slid back and she threw the door open.

Walter was standing by the counter in the booking-in area, waiting for our arrival.

"Cell 5. Something's wrong. I think he's having a seizure or something."

We walked quickly to Cell 5. Its occupant, Scabby, was lying peacefully on his bunk, covered head to foot with a grey wool blanket. Although we could not see his body, the blanket twisted and jerked as though he was in the midst of a seizure.

"Anybody got any idea if this guy's an epileptic or something?" Denis asked. "He sure is making funny breathing sounds."

We looked on the twitching blanket for a few seconds. Suddenly, Ruth grabbed the key from the guard and threw open the door. Grabbing the blanket by its corner, she tossed it aside. Scabby had torn a strip from his shirt and looped it around his neck. Using his wrist as a pivot, he had tightened the ligature until his carotid artery was compressed enough to restrict blood-flow to his brain.

119

"It's a horizontal hanging," Ruth said, once again using her policy-forbidden knife to cut through the cloth. "Grab his legs!" she shouted. Denis grabbed Scabby's legs and Ruth lifted his shoulders from the steel bunk. Together, they carried him to the hallway.

Our next step was the stuff nightmares are made from.

"I'll call an ambulance!" Walt shouted as he ran for the telephone.

"Use 9-1-1!" Ruth called back.

"Okay, what's their number?" Walt briefly shook his head. We half-laughed at the confusion, then he disappeared around the corner.

"I got the chest compressions!" I said, feeling for a non-existent carotid pulse.

"You're a dead man, Teather. I'll get you for this," Ruth said, as she tilted Scabby's head back and opened his airway. She gave three puffs into Scabby's mouth, vomited on the floor beside him, then continued.

"One thousand and one. One thousand and two." I counted out loud as I compressed his breastbone. When I had reached one thousand and five I paused while Ruth inflated his lungs.

Over my shoulder, I could hear Denis retching.

"Play the game or get off the field!" Ruth called sarcastically to the Sergeant. To my surprise, Denis knelt on the other side and took his turn, inflating Scabby's lungs and vomiting on the floor with Ruth.

Five minutes later our saviours arrived. Dressed in white shirts and navy blue pants, carrying oxygen, airways and stethoscopes, they took over the unpleasant task.

Running nonstop to the small kitchen located in the cell block, Ruth and Denis banged heads over the sink. For the next five minutes they splashed water on their faces, rinsed their mouths out, gargled, then repeated the process.

Denis was more of a man than I had ever given him credit for.

Barely had the mouth-rinsing Olympics drawn to a close when Bill Heckler, one of our finest paramedics, stuck his head into the kitchen.

"He's gonna be all right, Bobo," he said. "We have him stabilized. Got a heartbeat and respiration. He's still unconscious but he's alive. We're going to transport him now." Then his greying hair and thin face disappeared around the corner.

Two minutes later, red and blue lights accompanied by a siren left our cell block for the same hospital that held Higgy's near-lifeless body.

120

"Here, try some of this. It's a better disinfectant than that green soap you've been using." Walter poured four cups of the world's strongest coffee. One was for himself.

"Thanks, Walt." Denis smiled then winced as he burned his lip on the hot liquid. "What would we ever do without you?"

We drank coffee and complimented ourselves on a job well done. Conversation turned to Wanda and Terry Dexter. Ruth and I filled in Sergeant Denis on the occurrence and told him about Rod and Frank.

"God how I envy you," he said, looking at both of us. "You're young, strong, brave and you still got the guts to get out there and work." Ruth looked at me and I could see one eyebrow rise higher than the other.

"I'm just an old burnt-out-fart," he continued. "I guess some days I'm kinda tough on you young squirts. Don't mean to be. Don't ever think I don't care 'cause I do." He looked down at his coffee. "Damn, I'm getting all mushy. Don't mean to. Look guys, I know what you've been through. Been there — done that myself. Won't bore you with the details. You did good. Just don't think I don't care."

"Don't worry about that, Sarge," I said, remembering the identity of the mysterious guardian angel that nurse Jane had told me about.

"I guess I'm just too old anymore." The Sergeant's finger circled an old scar on his left forearm. I had never noticed it before. It was a small circular scar on the top and bottom of his forearm. I had seen similar scars before. It was unmistakable. A gunshot wound.

We finished our coffee and left the cell block, thanking Walt for his vigilance. He was our best prison guard, part of our family.

Together we sat, sharing a long table. Forms, paper and pens littered its surface. But our report writing was to be disturbed. Constable Stewart Dudzinski entered the room.

"Hey, Dudz!" Ruth called out. Stewart was carrying a large box. "Whatchya got there?" she asked.

"Exhibits," he said. "Got them from an old car I found up in Whalley. Funniest thing ever. Had a V-shaped crack in the windshield, the front passenger door didn't work, and look at this!" He held up a tiny gold butterfly-shaped figure. "Think Scooter might want this back?" His smile grew until it reached both ears. Then he added, "Know where Bev is?"

"She ought to be around here somewhere." I thought for a moment. "Last heard her go 10-7 with Martha. Haven't heard her go back on the air yet." Even when we were in the police station, we kept our portables on. They usually worked well enough to cover the short distance to and from the parking lot. I had not heard Bev clear from the office. I reasoned she must be somewhere in the complex.

Reaching for a telephone, Stewart punched 8-3. "Bev to the Constable's room please." His voice was electronically projected into every room of the police station except our Chief's room. He usually had his speaker turned off.

"Hi, guys! Sorry 'bout Terry, I caught most of it from the radio room...."

Stewart cut her off. The Terry episode was history. His thoughts and actions were focused on catching a brutal rapist. He looked at Bev. "You still got that rubber cup you found by the dump?

"Sure do."

"Go get it."

Two minutes later Bev appeared with the cup, still sealed in its exhibit bag. Dudzinski leaned forward and focused his eyes intently on its contents.

"Good work, Bev. Just set it on the table."

Dudzinski carefully studied it, then slowly pointed with the index finger of his right hand. "One tiny hair. I wonder what little blonde girl this belongs to?" We all drew near to see the hair.

"What is it?" Bev asked.

"A hair, dummy!" Stewart replied.

"No, the cup. What is it?"

Dudzinski waved his arms wide for the benefit of an imaginary crowd. "And now, ladies and gentlemen, for 'la piece de resistance.' He tried his best to mimic a French accent. Reaching down he pulled an old bamboo cane from the box and pointed to its bottom. It was obvious that something was missing. The cane was dirty, scratched and weathered — except for the bottom two inches. Holding the cane's tip against the rubber cup, still sealed in Bev's exhibit bag, Dudzinksi said, "Think it fits? Green wiener!" He broke into a smile and we all laughed.

Dudzinski had coined the expression "green wiener" one night while playing poker. He had bluffed his opponent and had successfully won the hand with a pair of deuces. Looking across the table he calmly announced "green wiener." His expression had stuck and from that day forth he would proudly use it to declare victory.

"That's a green wiener for sure!" Bev agreed.

Dudzinski had done it again. In one short shift, he had seized the crime vehicle and directed us toward the crime scene. There was only one thing left to do.

Arrest the suspect.

"Hey, you guys gonna get some work done or just stand

around talking!" Denis called from the doorway. "Ruth, you got some work to do on Scabby. Let's get the forms on my desk before the end of shift or you'll miss the big party."

"Scabby?" Stewart shouted. "You seen Scabby? Where the hell is he?"

Ruth explained the incident that had just transpired in the cellblock, complete with a full description of her stomach contents on the tile floor and the foul tasting coffee that Walt had brewed us.

Stewart half-sat, half-collapsed into a chair. "Scabby, you little piece of puke."

"Explain," Ruth invited him to continue.

"I just don't believe it."

"Explain," Bev added.

"Okay. I might as well. It goes like this." Stewart motioned for us to sit down. Rod and Frank had joined the group. "Let's take a look at what Scooter told you, Bev." She pulled out her notebook and reviewed its contents.

"You see, police work isn't knowing the street map," Stewart spoke the words to Frank. "It's knowing faces and names. Your head has to be a filing cabinet full of index cards. You just pump in the information and out pops the solution." Dudzinski reached out and looked at Bev's notes.

"We all know Scabby, most of us have arrested him. Let's put it all together." We listened intently.

"Scooter said her attacker mumbled, like her Dad when he drank too much but she did not smell booze, did she?"

"No," Bev answered.

"Okay. What did she smell?"

"Socks." Bev suggested.

"And?"

"Um, cleaning fluid or paint." She retrieved her notebook from Dudzinski and read from her notes.

"Okay. What does Scabby, alias Houseman, smell like?"

"Socks."

"And?"

"He's a glue sniffer," Ruth said. "When he can't get glue, he buys acetone, gasoline or paint thinner!"

And, Bev added, "He talks like he's drunk. He fried his brains years ago."

"Bingo." Stewart licked his forefinger and gave the girls one point on an imaginary scoreboard.

"Nobody — nobody, smells and talks like that." Stewart summarized. He sat back in his chair. "Now for the big one. Where does he live?" We were all silent.

"C'mon guys, don't be so dumb! Where does he live?"

Vaguely, I remembered coming across Scabby several months ago. He was asleep in a big, old.... "In his car!" I shouted. "The smelly little animal lives in his car!"

"And you never bothered to run the R.O. did you, Bob. You thought that old rust-bucket was an abandoned car. You never bothered to see if Scabby was the Registered Owner, did you? I bet you didn't even remember all the Cracker Jack boxes in his car! Like most addicts, Scabby lives on sweets. Remember the sticky boxes Scooter told you about? I bet you didn't even put that together, did you?"

"No, I didn't," I admitted.

"Police work, Frank." Stewart looked into the eyes of our new recruit then in a loud voice, added, "Police work!" Stewart tapped his forehead with his finger.

"Scabby is one glue-sniffing, gutter-crawling piece of slime." Then he added, "Think we got an I.D. or what!"

"Ya. Scooter will identify him," Bev said. "But why, Dudz, why didn't you tell us about him."

Stewart's face grew serious. Quietly, he spoke. "'Cause I wanted first crack at him. I wanted revenge. Okay? I wanted revenge! I wanted to ram his teeth so far down his throat he'd have to sit on his plate to eat. Just for once in my life I wanted revenge."

Stewart was serious. Dead serious. "I wanted to even the score for all the little Scooters in the world that had been hurt by this piece of vomit and others like him. I just wanted to even the score. No witnesses. Just me and him."

But it was too late.

We had just saved his life.

A hush fell upon us as we realized what we had done. We felt confused, dirty, sickened. We had saved the life of a half-human who had just destroyed an innocent young girl.

We had done our duty. And we would have to live with that simple fact.

Lyle Houseman, alias Scabby, was remanded in custody. Two years later, his trial and all its subsequent appeals were exhausted and he was sentenced to nine years in a Federal Penitentiary. Since it would take two years for his case to reach completion, he would be eligible for parole in one more year — one-third of his sentence.

Somewhere, within the Halls of Justice, a psychiatrist would declare that Houseman was too brain-damaged to be a repeat offender.

His parole would be recommended.

He would be free to offend again.

And he would!

124

CHAPTER 13

FREE COFFEE - FOR LIFE

I WILL NEVER FEAR TOMORROW,
FOR I HAVE SEEN YESTERDAY
AND SURVIVED TODAY.

I left my friends behind. Stacks of papers remained in front of them and they were busy completing forms. Coroner's forms, exhibit forms, crime reports, and even forms to request more forms when they ran out.

Bev and Rod had both suggested that my time would be better spent visiting Bruce. They understood how I felt and ushered me out of the office, promising to complete the paper work in my absence.

Fifteen minutes later I sat beside my fallen friend's near-life-less body.

Sitting in the hard aluminum chair, I drew close to Bruce. I told him about today's shift and how lucky he was to have missed it. I told him about the great Chicken Raid; I fought back tears and told him about Terry Dexter and his suicide; about Scooter and Scabby, and I told him how we missed him. Then in the quiet of the hospital room I said I was sorry. I was sorry for not lying in his bed. He had taken a beating that fate had intended for me. There was nothing I could do to turn back time and I regretted it.

Then I tried something I had not done for a long time. I prayed.

It was a hopeless prayer. Bruce showed no signs of recovery.

But I prayed anyway. And while in prayer, I remembered a card from the Deck.

Miracles are not contrary to nature.
Miracles are only contrary to what we know about nature.

I prayed for a miracle.

The sound of footsteps off to my right told me that nurse Jane had entered the room. I looked at her.

"There's been no change, Bob," she said. "I think I saw him move a finger a while ago, but the doctor says that doesn't mean anything."

125

"You ever heard that sometimes unconscious people can hear us talk?" I asked.

"Sure. That's what they say anyway. According to what I've read, they sometimes remember lots of things. Conversation, pain, being moved, smells, especially smells — lots of things."

I leaned close to Bruce's face. "If I said, 'Higgy, if you wake up now I'll buy you coffee for the rest of your life. If you don't I'll lay a beating on you so bad there'll be nothing left on this bed 'cept a pair of hospital pajamas,' do you think he'd hear me?"

"Sure would hope so," Jane said.

"Good," I tried to force a smile. "Please call me if there's any change. Here's our dispatch number, the White House number and my home. Please?"

"Okay, Bob. I'll call you and that Denee guy. I'll also pass it on to Dr. Harrington. He seems to have a special interest in Higgy as well. Says he'll be up here later to check with me."

"Oh," I said, "one more thing?"

"Yes?"

"Is the coffee on?"

"Sure! Want a cup?"

"Please."

A minute later Jane appeared with a cup of black coffee.

"Thanks, Jane." I quietly returned to Higgy's room and left the coffee on his bedside table. "Maybe the smell will wake you up, Higgy."

"Nice try, Bob," Jane said, as I walked from his room.

Back in my police car I called dispatch. "Bravo 23's clear of S.M.H., I'm R.T.O. and off shift."

"10-4 Bravo 23, see you at the party."

It was now 1900 hours, 7:00 p.m. by civilian time. It had been a long shift and I hoped I would never experience a similar one. Once in a lifetime was more than enough.

Time now to go home, change and join Sergeant Schlitz's retirement party.

The White House had been prepared for our old Sergeant's farewell party. Streamers were hung, balloons inflated and the doors propped wide open.

"C'mon, Frank, you ain't never been to the White House before," Rod stated.

Everyone had showered and put on clean clothes and made the short walk across the rear parking lot to the small, old wartime house that had been renovated into a recreation hall.

Rod and Frank led the procession. Ruth and Bev followed. Gord Schneider and I walked behind, still talking about Cuddles,

126

the Big White Lump. Even Bill Heckler, our favorite paramedic, and his new assistant joined the parade.

Sharon followed a few minutes later with Logan and Patti, the three best dispatchers of the entire detachment. Dispatchers were also part of our family. They could not stop a bullet for us, nor could they even offer us cover fire, but through their cool-headedness, our safety was ensured. They did share with us, however, our happiness and our pain.

Buffy Burton, a senior Constable who many years ago had been my trainer, also joined the group. He was known for his "stick-your-tongue-in-a-plug-socket" hairdo which drove our Sergeant half-crazy, but he was a good cop. With him, he brought the last few stragglers and we all waited for our guest of honor.

Sergeant Schlitz was ushered into the White House by our new Sergeant, Denis. He was clearly happy. He had just finished his retirement holidays and when the clock struck midnight, he would be Mr. Sterling Schlitz.

But we would always call him Sarge. He had earned the title.

"Hooray!" A cheer went up as our old Watch Commander walked through the door.

"You guys cheering 'cause I'm leaving?" he asked.

Laughter greeted his remark. Then Rod said, "Sarge, before you leave us, and we all forget your name...." We all laughed. No one would ever forget Sterling. No one. "As I was saying, here's a little something we've bought to remember us by." Rod handed the packages to Sergeant Denis. It was fitting for the gift to be offered by his new replacement.

"Aw shucks, guys. You shouldn't have." Schlitz mocked us.

Opening the packages, Schlitz acknowledged the obligatory pewter beer stein, complete with his name, regimental number and RCMP crest. He also held up the Detachment's gift — a plaque. The RCMP crest once again mounted over his name, regimental number and dates of service.

"Then there's something special here we'd like you to have." Denis offered a small package to Sterling. "It comes from all of us. I know it's against policy, but after what I saw today, I hope we will all have one from now on."

Slowly, Sterling opened the box. Inside was a knife. Not just any knife, but a lock-knife complete with sheath. Unlike any knife worn by any of the Watch, however, this one was made from titanium. It was so light it felt like plastic and so strong it would outlive its owner. Inscribed on the side was:

"TO STERLING SCHLITZ - THE BEST COP EVER"

Sterling's eyes filled with tears as he held up his gift. He tried to talk. At first, he was unsuccessful. Then he cleared his throat and managed a simple, short and from-the-heart, "Thanks, guys."

We cheered.

"Thanks a lot."

The room exploded into more cheers. Everyone raised a glass of beer to the man they had called friend, and, as the evening progressed, Sergeant Denis was finally accepted into the Watch.

The party continued. Music played. We danced, told jokes, drank, then told more jokes. Our parties were like that.

Later that evening, the music played slow and we all sat around trading stories. Somewhere in between stories, Martha Kruntz, Cuddles and Terry Dexter made an appearance. Then, as the hours wore on, the room grew quiet while we listened to each other's stories. Stories of mirth and mischief, of heroism and death. Stories that told us who we were.

Somewhere amidst the stories, the telephone rang. Ruth rose to answer it. She spoke for about a minute, then walked into the center of the room.

"I've a message for you, Bob." She spoke slowly and the room fell silent. "It's from Dr. Harrington. He says he has a message which he promised to pass on." Her eyes did not leave mine.

The room remained silent.

"Higgy says, 'Next time, I want double sugar and double cream, and if you ever threaten me like that again ... you had better bring some back-up'."

Time stopped. Everyone in the room sniffled. Sterling Schlitz tried to speak but couldn't. Our eyes met briefly, then filled with tears.

I don't remember much. The room was quite blurry. Then, softly, someone began to sing:

> *Should auld acquaintance be forgot*
> *and never brought to mind....*

We all joined in.

128